DARE
WE SEEK
YOU

DAILY WE SEEK YOU

REFLECTIONS AND PRAYERS FOR INDIVIDUALS, CAREGIVERS AND MINISTRY TEAMS

JANE McCONNELL, O.S.F.

Outskirts Press, Inc.
Denver, Colorado

Daily We Seek You
Reflections and Prayers for Individuals, Caregivers and Ministry Teams
All Rights Reserved.
Copyright © 2012 Jane McConnell, O.S.F., with Sisters of St. Francis, Oldenburg, IN
v3.0

Outskirts Press, Inc.
http://www.outskirtspress.com

ISBN: 978-1-4327-8165-1

Outskirts Press and the "OP" logo are trademarks belonging to Outskirts Press, Inc.

PRINTED IN THE UNITED STATES OF AMERICA

Dedication

This book is lovingly dedicated to my parents,
William and Jessie (Yeager) McConnell,
who celebrate their 90th birthdays
and their 70th wedding anniversary this year.
Their faithful love and dedication to each other,
and their love, support, and encouragement
to me and to all our family have been an inspiration
beyond what words can describe.
They have shared their presence and loving care
with us through all the joys and struggles of our lives.
They were the ones who first shared faith,
family and Christian values,
and the spirit of prayer with each of us.
I am eternally grateful for the gift of life and love
they have given to me.
Thank you, Mom and Dad!

Table of Contents

Foreword..i
Introduction...v

Section I   Daily Reflections and Prayers.....................................1

                  January...3
                  February...17
                  March 29
                  April...43
                  May..55
                  June...69
                  July..83
                  August..97
                  September 111
                  October..125
                  November 139
                  December 153

Section II   Other Prayer Resources for
                Individual or Group Use 167

                Prayers for Other Times Along Life's Journey 169
                Monthly Gathering Prayers 183
                  Letting God Speak to Us
                in Times of Anxiety or Illness 199

Index...205

Foreword

"There is no way I can adequately express my gratitude to Sister Jane for her dedication to religious life and her hospital ministry with St. Mary's Health System. Sister Jane has 'been there and done that'. She suffered intensely. She underwent painful rehabilitation after a most serious car accident. She is a walking miracle. Her reflections and prayers flow from the depths of her heart. She is a most compassionate woman of faith and a dedicated Religious Sister of the Order of St. Francis of Oldenburg, Indiana. She epitomizes the spirit of St. Francis of Assisi. She cares for the suffering and disenfranchised. She has been such a gift to the Catholic Diocese of Evansville. She gives her compassionate heart to all she meets. That is a special gift from which we all benefit. Please give serious consideration to her request for the publication of her efforts on behalf of those who are suffering illness and pain, even facing death."

+ Bishop Gerald Gettelfinger, Evansville Diocese (retired 2011)

"Sister Jane has been an Oldenburg Franciscan for 46 years. Her dedication in any ministry she has held has been outstanding. Her present ministry with St. Mary's Health System has given her the opportunity to reach out to those who suffer in many ways. She has also shared her love, spirituality, and giftedness with co-workers, giving them the courage to continue to be a Christ presence to those in their care. Sister Jane is a dynamic, joyous, and enthusiastic witness of God's presence among us. Sister Jane's creativity and spirituality permeate her prayers. These prayers come from her lived experience. It would be a gift to our world to have these prayers in print so that those who suffer or struggle with difficult life situations can be reminded of God's loving presence in their life. Please give serious consideration to Jane's request for the publication of her prayers for those who suffer and for their care-givers."

Sister Barbara Piller, Congregational Minister
Sisters of St. Francis, Oldenburg, Indiana

"Sister Jane McConnell's Daily Reflections and Prayers, Gathering Prayers and seasonal prayers are ongoing inspiration and support to me in my role of Director of Nursing at St. Mary's Medical Center. They motivate me to find creative and innovative ways to serve others and to become a better person. The Daily Reflections and Prayers are short but meaningful and I take time in my schedule each day to read and reflect upon their message and upon how I can incorporate that into my day and my life. The Gathering Prayers are reflective of the month or season and especially geared toward opening a department or team meeting. Using the imagery of the seasons, they help us visualize how we can serve others better. The seasonal reflections and prayers are educational as well as inspirational. I highly endorse Sister Jane McConnell and her effort to publish her work. I would cherish such a book and feel others would as well.

Penny Bodkin, RN, BSN,NE-BC
Director Same Day Surgery/Pre Procedure Clinic
St. Mary's Medical Center, Evansville, IN

"I am writing a letter of endorsement for Sr. Jane McConnell who is the Director of Mission Integration for St. Mary's Health System in Evansville, IN. The health system includes St. Mary's Medical Center, inpatient and outpatient services and medical offices for employed physicians and their staffs. Sister Jane publishes on the hospital e-mail system a daily reflection under the title Spirituality in the Workplace, SM. This e-mail goes out to well over three thousand employees each morning including weekends. They are short and concise in their message – a message directed toward health care workers. A book of Sister's meditations has been proposed and I can't tell you what a gift that would be especially if it were made available to our patients. I am unaware if these daily reflection are now read by patients, but I do know that the message put forth tries to set the "spiritual" tone for us who interact with patients and staff. Although geared toward the health care provider, I believe patients would be helped by these meditations. We need to recognize the need for spiritual healing as well as for a physical healing. I am not sure we can claim a treatment success if one or both of these entities is given limited attention. Sister has a gift of communicating to us in a way that brings to mind why we chose to go into the health care field in the first place. These daily reminders are not only important but are in my estimation absolutely needed to maintain our focus and direction. I would ask that you give strong consideration to publishing a book of these meaningful meditations for health care workers and those they care for."

Peter Rosario, MD
St. Mary's Medical Center
Evansville, Indiana

Introduction

After serving in a faith-based acute care hospital setting as a Chaplain for nine years and now as Director of Mission Integration for four years, I have found employees and leadership desiring to have resources available to them for Prayer and Reflection for personal use and staff meeting times. As a Chaplain, I wrote several prayer resources which were used by our staff and also placed in our Chapel for those who may visit or seek a place of quiet for reflection, comfort, and strength. Now as Director of Mission Integration, I have been writing Daily Reflections and Prayers, Monthly Gathering Prayer, and other seasonal reflection resources which are sent by e-mail to all in our health system (St. Mary's Health System, Evansville, IN) for their individual or staff use.

Several physicians, our previous CFO, and many employees have told me that the first thing they do in the morning, as they begin their work, is to open the Daily Reflection and Prayer in their e-mail. They have told me this brief resource helps them to focus their day and center themselves for the work and ministry they are about to begin. One physician told me that when things get hectic through the day, he goes to his office, closes the door and reopens the Daily Reflection and Prayer e-mail to help him re-focus and center himself again. Other employees have told me they have shared these with friends and family members, who have found these helpful to use for personal prayer and reflection each day.

It is for these reasons that I have been encouraged to compile many of the reflection and prayer resources which I have written and offer them for publication. My hope is that many who serve as healthcare workers, caregivers, on ministry teams, or who seek individual time for quiet and reflection will find these resources helpful in nurturing their own spirits and encouraging their hearts, as they give so generously of themselves serving others in need. I pray that this will be true for you as you open this book, <u>Daily We Seek You,</u> and use the reflections and prayers provided.

Sister Jane McConnell, OSF
September 8, 2011

Section I
Daily Reflections and Prayers

January

January 1

REFLECTION

As the gift of this New Year begins, what in me needs renewing so that I may live in peace, in good health, and in gratitude for all the blessings I have been given?

PRAYER

God of new beginnings, with the rising of the sun and the coming of light each morning, You offer each of us the chance to be new and to start again. Bless our efforts toward living in peace, being healthy and wholesome, and living with an attitude of gratitude throughout this New Year. Amen

January 2

REFLECTION

The uncertainties of the present can give way to the wondrous possibilities of the future. How do I hold and deal with the uncertainties which life presents? Do I step forward in hope and trust to let the positive possibilities unfold?

PRAYER

Loving God, as we face the uncertainties which come to us on our journeys in life, help us be reminded to trust in Your guidance and direction. Assist us to have patience and wisdom in knowing when to act and when to wait. Amen

January 3

REFLECTION

If we love one another, God remains in us, and God's love is brought to perfection in us. *(1 John 4:12)* How will God's love be brought to perfection in me today?

PRAYER

Life-giving God, teach me self-less and generous love as I serve Your people each day. Give me an understanding heart and a non-judgmental spirit as I work with others to assist my sisters and brothers in their time of need.

January 4

REFLECTION

Give something, however small, to the one in need. For it is not small to one who has nothing. Neither is it small to God, when we have given what we could. What may God be asking me to give and share with someone today?

PRAYER

God, even if it seems I have nothing extraordinary or special to give today, help me to give a smile, an encouraging word, a gesture of kindness, the gift of presence, and then let You use these things to help others. Amen

January 5

REFLECTION

Have you ever had a surprising spiritual experience that you felt was like a little glimpse of heaven? Simple everyday joys and spiritual experiences can slip by unnoticed if we only rush through our day. How can I pace myself today to let God bless me with these special gifts being offered?

PRAYER

God-with-us, just as the three Magi were attentive to the changes in the night sky and the movement of the stars; help us to slow the pace of our lives in order to see the subtle and quiet signs of Your presence and direction for us. May Your light and message guide our path and our decisions each day. Amen

January 6

REFLECTION

Today we remember and celebrate the journey of the Magi, who followed a bright star guiding them in faith through unfamiliar territory, to find the Christ Child born in Bethlehem. *(Matthew 2:1-12)* What is the guiding light which gives me direction in my own journey of faith? In what ways do I seek and follow this light each day?

PRAYER

Faithful God, we desire to be attentive to the light and direction You give to us each day as we walk our journey in life. Open our eyes to all the "epiphanies" and new awakenings which You place in our lives. Amen

January 7

REFLECTION

Moments of unconditional love for another can sometimes flow out of us and even surprise us as they happen. When these moments happen, we can know that we are living inside a Larger Life than our own… the Larger Life of God. In what ways might I find myself living in the Larger Life of God today as I serve and care for others?

PRAYER

God, Light to all the nations, guide my thoughts and actions each day that all I am and all I do may contribute to the larger plan of life and goodness You desire for all people and all creation. May all I do today bring hope and healing to those around me. Amen

January 8

REFLECTION

The Spirit of God is upon me because the Lord has anointed me to bring glad tidings to the poor; to heal the brokenhearted; to proclaim liberty to captives and release to prisoners; and to proclaim a year of favor from the Lord. *(Isaiah 61:1-2)* What special "anointing" might God be gifting me with today? How will I respond?

PRAYER

Anointing God, help us to be aware of Your message and call in our lives today. Guide us to know how to bring hope, healing, relief, and the promise of Your love to all those we encounter each day. Amen

January 9

REFLECTION

We become holy not by our own efforts to overcome our weaknesses, but by letting God give us the strength and purity of God's Spirit in exchange for our own weakness and misery. *(Thomas Merton)* What do I need from God today?

PRAYER

Gracious God, You are the light in our darkness. Guide us to rely on Your mercy, Your compassion, Your strength as You free us and renew us to live in Your ways of goodness and truth. Amen

January 10

REFLECTION

The Spirit of the Lord is upon me, because he has anointed me to bring glad tidings to the poor. He has sent me to proclaim liberty to captives and recovery of sight to the blind, to let the oppressed go free, and to proclaim a year of favor for the Lord. *(Luke 4:18-19)* What is God calling me to do today for someone?

PRAYER

Liberating God, let me feel Your anointing in my life and be directed by Your call to assist others who are seeking to be free of their burdens and whatever may be oppressing them. Make me an instrument of Your Peace and Loving Kindness for others. Amen

January 11

REFLECTION

Through God's Holy Spirit hearts are raised up, the weak are led by the hand, and those who are making progress are encouraged. How will I know God's touch in my life today and how will I be a healing touch for others?

PRAYER

Life-Giving Spirit of God, raise me up when I falter, lead me always by Your hand, encourage me in my times of need so that my life and ministry can be life-giving and supportive to others. Amen

January 12

REFLECTION

The Scriptures remind us that God often guides the actions and good works of those we may least expect or look to as we go through our day. Who have I noticed doing God's work, sharing God's goodness in unexpected ways?

PRAYER

Ever-Present God, open our eyes and stretch our narrow vision that we may see You present in the actions, kindness, suggestions, and unselfish giving of those around us today… especially in the ways and times we may least expect. Amen

January 13

REFLECTION

The human heart has its own memory, like the human mind. In the heart are held precious keepsakes and gratitude for the giver's loving kindness. What precious keepsakes will others hold in their hearts from my interactions with them today?

PRAYER

Life-Giving God, guide our actions and words so that all we do may lift up and encourage those we serve and work among each day. Amen

January 14

REFLECTION

We should strive to keep our hearts open to the suffering and struggles of other people, and pray continually that God may grant us that spirit of compassion which is truly the spirit of God. *(St. Vincent de Paul)* How aware will I be today of the suffering and struggles of others… the spoken and the unspoken?

PRAYER

God of Compassion, lift us beyond our own needs and concerns today so that we may truly see the suffering and struggles of others and attend to them with kindness and compassion. Amen

January 15

REFLECTION

A leper came to Jesus and kneeling down begged him and said, "If you wish, you can make me clean." Jesus reached out his hand, touched the leper, and said to him, "I do will it. Be made clean." *(Mark 1:40-41)* What in me needs to be healed, made new, or refreshed in this New Year?

PRAYER

Healing and Renewing God, You offer every day as a new beginning for each of us. Guide us to know ourselves and become open to the opportunities You call us to for change and renewal. Amen

January 16

REFLECTION

Some came bringing to Jesus a paralytic carried by four men. Unable to get near Jesus because of the crowd, they opened up the roof above Jesus and let down the mat on which the paralytic was lying. *(Mark 2:3-4)* When you are tired, discouraged or "paralyzed" in some way, who are the four people you can count on to help "carry", support or care for you?

PRAYER

Gracious God, thank You for those faithful friends You have put into my life who help to "carry", support, and care for me during difficult times. Thank You for being my Faithful and True Friend each day also. Amen

January 17

REFLECTION

God has given each of you some special abilities; be sure to use them to help each other, passing on to others God's many varied blessings. *(1 Peter 4:10)* How might God use me as a special instrument for good today?

PRAYER

Generous and Gracious God, thank You for the unique abilities and talents You have given to each of us. Guide us to appreciate, develop, and share these gifts for the common good in our work and relationships. Amen

January 18
Week of Prayer for Christian Unity

REFLECTION

I pray that they all may be one, as you Father and I are one. May they all be one in us. *(John 18:20-21)* Each year the Church community invites us to a special week of praying for Christian Unity. How do I promote unity among my Christian sisters and brothers, among all God's people, through my attitudes, welcome, and the respect I give to each person I meet?

PRAYER

God of heaven and earth, hear our prayers, and show us the way to peace, unity, and mutual respect among all people of our world, our local communities, and our families. Amen

January 19

REFLECTION

How open am I to the faith traditions and journeys of those I interact with at work, in my neighborhood, in our world? In what ways am I enriched by the diversity of life, religious practice and faith they live and share?

PRAYER

Creator God, guide us that we may see all persons as our brothers and sisters created in Your image and likeness. May we be strengthened and enriched by the spirituality and faith of each person we meet today. Amen

January 20

REFLECTION

Life is what we are alive to notice, receive, and give. It is not measured merely in length of time. Be alive to goodness, kindness, integrity, love, history, poetry, music, flowers, stars, God, and eternal hope.

PRAYER

Generous God, in the gift of each new day You give us opportunities to be more fully alive. Help us to be fully alive today to the beauty of another person's goodness, to kindnesses shared, to music which lifts our spirits, and most of all to Your life-giving presence within us and among us. Amen

January 21

REFLECTION

I thank God for you whenever I think of you. As I remember you, I pray with joy in my heart. *(Philippians 1:3-4)* How often do I pray for my co-workers, asking God to bless them with Peace and All Good as we begin and continue through our day?

PRAYER

Life-Giving God, bless each of us with what we will need to serve You and all Your people who come to us in need of healing, kindness, encouragement, and hope this day. Amen

January 22

REFLECTION

Jesus asked his disciples to have a boat ready for him because of the crowd… He had cured many and, as a result, those who had diseases were pressing upon him to touch him. *(Mark 3:9-10)* Do you ever feel crowded or pressed by time or all the needs around you at work or in your family? Ask God to guide you at times like these with patience and wisdom.

PRAYER

Gracious God, grant to each of us the patience and wisdom we will need this day to serve well all those who come to us. Help us to take a few quiet moments apart to seek the harmony and inner peace we need to stay healthy and kind. Amen

January 23

REFLECTION

An act of love, a voluntary taking on oneself some of the pain of the world, can increase the courage and love and hope of all. *(Dorothy Day)* How might I be called today to take on or be with another person in their suffering or pain? How will I respond in love?

PRAYER

God of Comfort, guide us to look beyond our own needs and our own comfort to relieve the suffering and pain of others we will meet this day. May the comfort and care we give, be a reflection of Your love and care for those in need. Amen

January 24

REFLECTION

You have not chosen me; I have chosen you. Go and bear fruit that will last. *(John 15:16)* Have you felt chosen by God for a special purpose or mission in life? How do you respond and also nurture this call in order to bear fruit that will last?

PRAYER

Ever-Present God, You invite us to walk the journey of life with You each day. Open our hearts to hear Your call in our lives. Open our spirits to respond and live with generosity and joy. Amen

January 25

REFLECTION

Your ways, O Lord, make known to me; teach me your paths, guide me in your truth and teach me, for you are God, my Savior. *(Psalm 25:4-5)* As I go through my day, do I nurture my inner spirit by pausing to ask God's guidance and direction in meeting the challenges and seeking God's ways?

PRAYER

Spirit of the Living God, guide me to seek and know Your truth and Your ways as I serve with and among Your people each day. May my actions and behaviors reflect Your compassion and loving presence to all. Amen

January 26

REFLECTION

I remind you to stir into flame the gift of God that you have received. For God did not give us a spirit of cowardice, but rather of power and love and self-control. *(2 Timothy 1:6-7)* What do I do each day, each week to nurture my inner spirit; to stir into flame the gifts God has given me to share in loving and self-giving ways?

PRAYER

Gracious and Generous God, show me ways to nurture my inner spirit and stir into flames the gifts You have given me. Enkindle in me a generous heart, a spirit of service which reflects Your goodness and love each day. Amen

January 27

REFLECTION

A good heart as well as a soul inflamed with charity will do good and holy works. *(St. Angela Merici)* What good and holy works might God be calling me to be a part of today? How might God use me as an instrument to touch and bring healing to another?

PRAYER

God of Wisdom and Love, send Your Spirit to guide our actions and teach us Your truth as we serve those in need today. Bless us with generosity of spirit as we minister with our co-workers each day. Amen

January 28

REFLECTION

One of the greatest things we can do for others is not just to share our riches with them, but also to reveal to them their own. How will I nurture the spirit and encourage the heart of another today?

PRAYER

God of Light, thank You for the goodness and blessings You have showered upon each of us. Guide us to share our own blessings and help others to see and appreciate their own as well each day. Amen

January 29

REFLECTION

We must consider how to rouse one another to love and good works. Join one another assembled in prayer and encourage one another. *(Hebrews 10:24-25)* How can we encourage one another today to love sincerely and work for the common good of all?

PRAYER

Thank You, God, for friends, family, and co-workers who model Your love and goodness. Thank You for those who rouse my heart and desire to know You and to be the best that I can be. Amen

January 30

REFLECTION

Happiness is an attitude. We either choose to be happy and strong, or to be miserable. The amount of effort is often the same. What is my attitude and perspective today? What choices will I make as I begin and continue through my day?

PRAYER

Ever-Present God, guide my attitude and my choices today. Help me to spend my efforts and energy in ways which bring joy, healing, hope, and encouragement to other persons each day. Amen

January 31

REFLECTION

Happiness comes of the capacity to feel deeply, to enjoy simply, to think freely, to enter the adventure of life, to be needed and to give ourselves unselfishly. We can't really capture or hold tight to happiness… it comes as a gift to those who are generous of heart.

PRAYER

Providential God, You shower each of us with a generous abundance of gifts and blessings every day. May we show our gratitude to You and live with joy and generous hearts. Amen

February

February 1

REFLECTION

Let your love be generous. Do not neglect hospitality, for through it some have unknowingly entertained angels. *(Hebrews 13:1-2)* Who might be an angel, a messenger of God, that I may be called to welcome today?

PRAYER

Gracious God, help us through our caring behaviors to share genuine warmth and hospitality to all we meet and interact with today. Amen

February 2

REFLECTION

The young couple, Mary and Joseph, bringing their child to pray in the temple, brought a surprising experience of God's revelation to Simeon and Anna. *(Luke 2:22-40)* Who might be an unexpected instrument of God's presence and revelation to me today?

PRAYER

God of Light, open our eyes and our hearts that we might be aware of the surprising and unexpected ways You reveal Yourself to us each day. Create in us the ability to receive and share Your message and Your presence in the ordinary events of life. Amen

February 3

REFLECTION

A prayer for healing and blessing of throats which is offered today dates back to the life of a Christian Bishop and Martyr, St. Blaise. He is remembered for saving the life of a small boy who had a fish bone obstructing his throat, and for bringing healing to others who suffered from illnesses of the throat. How might God use me to bring a healing touch or comforting presence to someone in need today?

PRAYER

Healing God, touch those in need today who are suffering with illnesses of the throat and all other illnesses. Guide each of us to be instruments of Your healing touch and hope for all we meet each day. Amen

February 4

REFLECTION

All of us at some time in our lives are in need of healing. Sometimes God reaches out to heal us directly, and sometimes God heals us through others. What special gifts of healing have you experienced in your life?

PRAYER

Ever-Present God, thank You for all the times and ways You bring healing and renewed strength to each of us. May all we do in our ministry of care reflect the compassion, comfort, and healing You desire to bring to those we serve. Amen

February 5

REFLECTION

Sometimes in life we may carry extra burdens or baggage, such as unhealthy attitudes, self-doubt, or a negative spirit within. When this happens, what do I do to choose life, to lay down the burden, and let God's spirit refresh my own? When we do this, our life and ministry can be more wholesome and productive.

PRAYER

Life-Giving God, free us from any burdens or baggage which weighs us down. Lead us to keep our vision clear, our hands and hearts free, to serve You and Your people in good and holy ways. Amen

February 6

REFLECTION

A vacation we often need is freedom from our own mind. Letting go of our obsessive thought patterns, our need to control events and other people can be our ticket to a relaxing beach, a restful waterfall, peace and calm in our own hearts. What restful "vacation" may God be inviting me to enjoy?

PRAYER

God of the Sabbath, You often invite us to "sabbath" times and moments in our week and in each day. Soften our hearts and free our minds that we can let go of those obsessive things which we chose to let bind us and which keep us less free as we live and serve in Your name. Amen

February 7

REFLECTION

In the Gospels, Jesus is often responding to a request of a person in need of healing, or from a relative of the person in need. He reaches out to touch them or they reach to touch him. What a privilege and an honor we have to continue the healing ministry of Jesus. How will I offer the healing touch of God today?

PRAYER

Compassionate God, guide our hands and our work that we may be instruments of Your healing care, Your healing touch for all we meet each day. Thank You for this ministry which You entrust to each of us. Amen

February 8

REFLECTION

Male and female, God created them. In God's image they were created. *(Genesis 1:27)* Do I respect my own life as being "created in the image of God"? Do I see and treat others with this same respect each day?

PRAYER

Creator God, on days when things get tough and the journey seems rough, I may lose sight of how and why You created me and continue to give me life. Help me to honor Your life within me and treat others with the same respect each day. Amen

February 9

REFLECTION

Anger is felt or expressed when an inner need or expectation is not being met or fulfilled. If I have felt anger recently, what need or expectation within me was not being met or fulfilled?

PRAYER

God of Truth and Life, when I feel angry, help me to pause, to reflect and become aware if I may be projecting on others my own expectations related to events in life or to fulfill my own inner needs. Guide me to inner peace. Amen

February 10

REFLECTION

We are all given great opportunities in life which may sometimes be disguised as impossible situations. How will we know when to welcome and step into the opportunities and when to let them pass?

PRAYER

Ever-Present God, as You walk the journey of life with us, open our eyes to recognize the opportunities which will bring life and hope along our way. Give us discerning and trusting hearts that we may embrace what is right and good as it comes to us. Amen

February 11
World Day of Prayer for the Sick

A PRAYER FOR THE CAREGIVERS

Faithful God, You are the source of strength and hope in our lives. Bless the healthcare settings where we work or visit, that these may be places of healing and compassion. Bless the people whom You have chosen to be instruments of Your healing, that they may be humble and skilled channels of Your grace. Where there is danger, may we protect life; where there is weakness and pain, may we provide relief and comfort; where there is anxiety and fear, may we offer gentle reassurances through our presence and kindness; and where all human efforts fail, may we be assured that we can rest secure in You. Bless all who work in healthcare with gentle and compassionate hearts, that they may find ways to live and model Your goodness. Bless all who come to them in need. Through their experience and care, may they be strengthened in their faith in You and gain new understandings in their lives. Amen

February 12

REFLECTION

Friendship, like immortality of the soul, may seem too good to be believed. When friendships are real, they are not glass threads or frostwork, but the solidest things we know. *(Ralph W. Emerson)* What friendships in your life have proven to be solid, true and nurturing to your soul? Celebrate and give thanks for these friendships -- gifts of God today.

PRAYER

God of Love, I thank You for the people You have placed in my life who are true and lasting friends. Thank You for the love they share with me, for the goodness and love they call forth from within me. Amen

February 13

REFLECTION

In the cultural time of the Hebrew Scriptures as well as New Testament times, people who were sick were often separated from the community due to fear or lack of knowledge about their disease. In our present time and culture, how can we help persons who are sick or suffering ill health feel more a part of the community, and not feel isolated?

PRAYER

God of Compassion, give us the openness and sensitivity of heart to be aware of those in our care and in our community who are ill or suffering and may feel alone or isolated. Guide us to find ways to help them feel included and welcomed. Amen

February 14

REFLECTION

The true and sure way to friendship is through humility – being open to each other, accepting each other as we are, growing to know each other, and leaving room for each other to grow and change. *(Mother Teresa of Calcutta)* How open, accepting, and humble am I in my relationships with others?

PRAYER

Creator God, thank You for Your acceptance of each of us as You created us. Open our eyes and our hearts to see the beauty and goodness in our co-workers and in all persons we are called to serve each day. Bless us with a spirit of humility and understanding in all we do. Amen

February 15

REFLECTION

Be on the lookout for God's blessings and mercies. The more we look for them, the more we will see them. How will God's blessings surprise and give joy to me today?

PRAYER

Merciful and Good God, open our eyes and our awareness to recognize and give thanks for Your blessings which come to us each day. Help us to see You present and acting in the ordinary events of our lives. Amen

February 16

REFLECTION

A single act of kindness gives out roots in all directions, and the roots spring up and nurture new life. In what direction will my actions and behaviors go today, and what kind of new life will come from them?

PRAYER

Creator God, direct our actions and behaviors today as we interact with our co-workers and all those we serve. May what we do and say each day bring positive energy and nurture new life for the common good. Amen

February 17

REFLECTION

Jesus has shown us in the Gospels not only that he heals, but also that we, as a community, are entrusted with the power to bring one another to healing. The kindness in our presence, our manner, and our touch can bring healing to another. How will this be true in my life today?

PRAYER

Gracious God, thank You for the healing You bring to each of our lives every day. Guide us to be instruments of Your comforting touch, Your healing presence for someone in need today. Amen

February 18

REFLECTION

Quiet moments of reflection and prayer may be the glue we need to hold our lives together each day. How do I make these a part of the routine or rhythm in my life? What small practices nurture my spirit?

PRAYER

Jesus, even in the business and demands You encountered each day, You modeled how important it is for us to "go apart and rest a while", to find time for quiet and prayer. Guide us to choose practices in our own lives which will nurture our spirits and keep us healthy and wise. Amen

February 19

REFLECTION

If the world and life seem cold or hum-drum to you, kindle the fires to warm it. What warmth or spark of life will I bring to my work and interactions today?

PRAYER

Life-Giving God, assist us to stir up the fires within us that will bring warmth, compassion, and healing to all those we serve with and touch each day. Melt and soften the places within us which may have become hardened or cold. Amen

February 20

REFLECTION

See, I am doing something new! Now it springs forth, do you not perceive it? *(Isaiah 43:19)* Is there something new or renewing God may desire to do in my life at this time? Do I have the eyes and the quietness of heart to perceive it and welcome it?

PRAYER

God of Wisdom, open us to feel and notice what it is in our lives that You may be desiring to renew or create as new. Heal our blindness and touch our hearts with Your mercy and compassion. Guide us to see as You see and to love as You love. Amen

February 21

REFLECTION

If you can't see what you're looking for, see what is before you. In the midst of our disappointments and unrealized dreams, we breathe and live in abundance. What blessings and goodness will I notice and give thanks for in my life today?

PRAYER

Ever-Present God, thank You for all the ways You provide for us each day. Give us a clear vision to see the blessings and abundant goodness You shower upon us today. Lead us to share these blessings with others and encourage them along life's journey. Amen

February 22

REFLECTION

What might I do during the Season of Lent to renew and refresh my relationship with God, with my family, co-workers, and my own inner spirit? In the Gospels, Jesus calls us to prayer, fasting, and sharing what we have with others.

God of Mercy and Compassion, guide us to renew ourselves and grow more in Your likeness during the days of the Lenten Season. May the signs of spring soon to come forth in nature around us, reflect the signs of new life and growth within us as well. Amen

February 23

REFLECTION

It has been observed that changing a habit or becoming rooted in a new virtue can happen with practice in 30 - 40 days. The Season of Lent is 40+ days. What am I hoping to change or have more rooted in my life during these days?

PRAYER

God of Mercy and New Life, guide us in the Season of Lent to let go of what burdens and weighs us down. Lead us to seek habits and virtues which renew our spirits and open us to serve those around us with generosity and joy. Amen

February 24

REFLECTION

The food I do not use could be given to those who are hungry. The garments hanging in my closet could be worn by persons in need. The shoes I do not wear could be used by someone who has none. How will I share with others from my abundance today?

PRAYER

Generous God, guide us to be gracious in our own giving each day. Whether we give of our time, our skills, our compassion, or our resources, help us to give with a generous and cheerful spirit. Amen

February 25

REFLECTION

The foolish person seeks happiness in the distance; the wise ones grow it under their feet. Do I pursue happiness in the distance, or do I help to create it where I am each day?

PRAYER

Faithful God, guide us to bring joy and goodness into the ordinary events and interactions of our day. Help us to grow happiness from the inside out as we live in service of You and Your people. Amen

February 26

REFLECTION

In the Gospel passage Matthew 4:1-11, Jesus is led into the desert where he prayed, fasted, and was tempted for 40 days. His temptations centered around the human desires of seeking more power, prestige, and possessions for oneself. Which of these temptations do I tend to struggle with the most in my life? What insecurities within me might be driving these?

PRAYER

Creator God, teach us the ways You call us to live in humility and truth. May the brokenness and human limitations of our own lives open us to recognize our insecurities which often drive our attitudes and behaviors. Show us how to live with greater trust in You each day. Amen

February 27

REFLECTION

When Abram felt uncertain about his future, God asked him to go outside to "Look up at the sky and count the stars, if you can". *(Genesis 15:5)* The endless number of stars and abundance of light in the sky represent God's blessings and presence in our lives. How will I count my blessings today?

PRAYER

Ever-Present God, thank You for the natural signs You place in our lives which remind us of the endless blessings You shower upon us every day. Help us to trust in Your present and providential care all along our way. Amen

February 28

REFLECTION

Whatever you did for one of these…you did for me. *(Matthew 25:40)* What we do for others each day is holy, for what we do for them, we do for the One who created them and lives in them. How will I welcome a stranger, clothe the naked, care for the ill, and feed the hungry today?

PRAYER

Sustaining God, when we are tired, weary, and feeling far from being holy, help us to remember that in our care-giving we are also serving You. Amen

March

March 1

REFLECTION

Forgiveness may help heal the past and also help to create a more pleasant future. Is there something in my relationship with another, in the events of life which happen to me, or something within myself I am being called to forgive? What steps will I take to do this?

PRAYER

Forgiving God, soften our hearts to experience and offer forgiveness. Free us of any burden which weighs us down and prevents us from living the fullness of life and love which You call us to enjoy and share. Amen

March 2

REFLECTION

In three words I can sum up everything I've learned about life: It goes on. *(Robert Frost)* As you go through life with its many experiences, struggles, and joys, what simple words of wisdom help you make it through?

God of Insight and Wisdom, guide us each day to pause, step back, and reflect on what is truly important in our lives and in the lives of those we serve. Help us to let go of the "extra baggage" which often drags us down, so that we might live with a clear vision and attitude. Amen

March 3

REFLECTION

We will be known forever by the tracks we leave. *(Native American Proverb)* What kind of "tracks" will I leave through my behaviors, words, and actions today? What "prints" will I leave on the hearts and minds of others?

PRAYER

God-with-us, You came to live and walk among us to show us the path of life and truth. Direct our actions, our words, and our behaviors so that what we leave with others will reflect Your goodness and compassion. Amen

March 4

REFLECTION

God measures our love neither by the multitude nor magnitude of our deeds, but by the manner in which we do them. *(St. John of the Cross)* What will be the manner and motivation of my actions and deeds today?

PRAYER

All Knowing God, purify my heart and my attitudes today. Guide my actions and behaviors so that all I do truly serves You and those You have placed in my care and my life. May my decisions support healthy relationships rather than personal achievement or gain. Amen

March 5

REFLECTION

Life is an echo; what you send out comes back to you. *(Chinese Proverb)* What good can I do today? Watch for the ways this goodness may come back to refresh and renew your own spirit as well.

PRAYER

Ever-Present God, it has been said, Joy is the echo of God's life in us. Give me a generous and compassionate heart so that I may learn to see as You see, understand as You understand, and love as You love. Amen

March 6

REFLECTION

While doing his daily work, tending his flock in the desert and mountain area, Moses was surprised to see a burning bush. As he drew near, Moses heard God call out to him from the bush telling him that he was standing on holy ground. *(Exodus 3:1-5)* In what way might God try to get my attention today to let me know that where I am is also "holy ground"?

PRAYER

Ever-present God, open our eyes, ears, and awareness today. Help us to see the "burning bushes" in our lives which call us to slow down and recognize Your presence and Your voice, letting us know that where we stand, work and live is truly holy ground, Amen

March 7

REFLECTION

We are called to reflect like mirrors the brightness of God, growing brighter and brighter as we are transformed into the image that we reflect; this is the work of God's Spirit in us. *(2 Corinthians 3:18)* In what ways will I be a mirror reflecting the likeness of God to another this week?

Transforming God, continue to create and imprint Your own image and likeness in us. Guide our actions and our decisions so that all the ways we serve and care for others will reflect Your compassion and love. Amen

March 8

REFLECTION

Happiness comes from within. It does not really depend so much on what we have, but rather on what kind of a person we truly are and how we reach out to those around us. Be aware today of when happiness wells up within you. How does it affect your day?

PRAYER

Life-Giving God, guide each of us today to think of others' needs more than our own. In the emptying of our own self-interests and need to achieve, may we discover the true and lasting happiness which will come. Amen

March 9

REFLECTION

One of the positive things about making a mistake or being wrong is seeing what we can learn from it and growing to be a better person. How do I usually handle my mistakes and try to learn from them?

PRAYER

Eternal God, as we live and work together, help us to acknowledge our limitations and the weaknesses of our human nature. Open us to learn and grow in the midst of our mistakes so that we may serve You and Your people with humble hearts. Amen

March 10

REFLECTION

Sometimes our best prayer may be not asking for what we think we want, but asking God to change our hearts or our perspective in order to see and understand more clearly what God is asking of us. In my prayer today, what will I ask for?

PRAYER

Transforming God, touch our hearts and minds each day so that we may see more clearly, love more tenderly, and serve with true understanding and compassion. Amen.

March 11

REFLECTION

A person growing in mature faith learns that we do not forgive just because we are supposed to forgive. We forgive because *we need to be healed* – to rid ourselves of the toxins of resentment or hate within us. In doing this we learn to be healthier. In what ways am I becoming more mature and healthy in my faith journey?

PRAYER

God of Wisdom, be with us each day as we seek to grow and mature in our faith. Help us to become healthy in our relationships with our family, co-workers and all those we serve. Touch the places within us which need to be healed. Amen

March 12

REFLECTION

Treasure the love and friendships you have with others. These have the potential to survive long after any material wealth or good health may diminish. Am I more task and achievement oriented or am I more relationship oriented?

PRAYER

God of Wisdom, help us each to seek balance and harmony in our lives so that what we give our lives to will bring true and lasting treasures. Amen

March 13

REFLECTION

Great minds discuss ideas, average minds discuss events, and small minds discuss people. *(Eleanor Roosevelt)* What is usually the focus and content of my conversations with others as I go through my day?

PRAYER

God of Life and Goodness, help us to bring hope, a positive attitude and kindness in our conversations and interactions each day. May our speech and behaviors reflect Your goodness and love in our lives and relationships. Amen

March 14

REFLECTION

When we love God with all our heart, with all our soul, with all our mind, with all our strength; and when we love our neighbor as our self....We are not far from the Kingdom of God. *(Mark 12:28-34)* How will I show my love in some small or practical way today?

PRAYER

God-with-us, thank You for the simple yet challenging words You speak to us in these words of Scripture. Free us from any self-centered ways of acting, and guide us to love You and others with a pure and generous spirit. Amen

March 15

REFLECTION

Do not be upset if things are not as you would want them to be for a long time to come. Do the little you can, very peacefully and calmly, so as to allow room for the guidance of God in our lives. *(St. Louise de Marillac)* What kinds of things tend to worry or upset me? What helps me let go and open myself to God's guidance in my life?

PRAYER

Ever-Present God, guide us to use the knowledge and information we have to act and make decisions in our lives for the good of all we serve. Teach us how to maintain an inner peace which allows room for Your guidance and wisdom to be experienced. Amen

March 16

REFLECTION

One way of knowing that it is the Spirit of God and not my own ego or compulsions speaking within me is to discern: Does what I am hearing and sensing urge me to broaden the scope and depth of my love for other people? When and how do I recognize the Spirit of God speaking to me?

PRAYER

Spirit of God, guide us each day to feel Your nudges, know Your voice, and follow the good You are inviting us to do for those we serve, our co-workers, our families, and all those You bring into our lives. Amen

March 17

REFLECTION

These things I warmly wish to you - Someone to love, some work to do, a bit o' sun, a bit o' cheer, and a guardian angel always near. *(An Irish Blessing)* How can I look upon all those I see today and wish them God's blessings in their lives?

PRAYER

Gracious God, thank You for the grace and blessings You shower upon all of us each day. Show us ways to share these with others in order to encourage their hearts and lift their spirits. "May the strength of God guide us, may the wisdom of God teach us, may the hand of God protect us, and may the Word of God direct us." Amen *(Prayer of St. Patrick)*

March 18

REFLECTION

We are called to be instruments of God's healing for persons we encounter each day. What small word or act might I do today to help another person heal? Who might be God's instrument of healing for me today?

PRAYER

Loving God, anoint us and make us instruments of Your peace, Your healing, Your understanding and kindness today. Amen

March 19

REFLECTION

In the Gospel, Joseph was willing to change his life, his way of understanding and acting when he received God's message in a dream. *(Matthew1:16-24)* How might God be inviting me to new understanding and changes in my life?

PRAYER

God of Surprises, open our hearts and our inner vision to recognize the ways You speak to us. Stretch us to be open to embrace the wisdom and understanding which will guide us to follow in Your ways. Amen

March 20

REFLECTION

Let the one among you who is without sin be the first to throw a stone at her. *(John 8:7)* We cannot raise a person up by calling them down. When thoughts of judging or talking in a negative way about another person come to me, do I stop to look into the mirror of my own life first?

PRAYER

Forgiving God, thank you for the mercy and forgiveness You pour upon us each day. Soften our own hearts so that we might offer this same mercy and forgiveness to others, especially when we have thoughts of judging them. Amen

March 21

REFLECTION

When one door of happiness closes, another opens; but often we look so long at the closed door that we do not see the one which has been opened for us. *(Helen Keller)* What new doors or opportunities may be opening in my life? How can I let go of something in the past so that I can see what is opening before me?

PRAYER

God, Ever-Present, Ever-New, help me to recognize the new doors You may be opening for me and embrace the new opportunities which may evolve. Guide me in the ways I may need to let go in order for new life to come. Amen

March 22

REFLECTION

It's good at times to ask God to refresh the dry places in our lives – our fears, our anxieties, our selfishness, our greed – with the waters of God's blessings. What in me may need to be refreshed with the waters of God's blessings today?

Renewing God, refresh the dry or broken places within me in this season of spring and new life. Let Your waters of blessing flow upon me and within me that I may serve You and Your people with a generous and pure heart. Amen

March 23

REFLECTION

Seek the Lord and his strength; seek always the face of the Lord. *(Psalm 104:4)* As I seek to know and see God present in my life, whose actions or face might reveal God to me today?

PRAYER

God-with-us, You reveal Yourself in the ordinary events and persons we encounter each day. Open our eyes and our hearts to seek and find You present and acting in our lives today. Heal any blindness within us which may prevent this from happening. Amen

March 24

REFLECTION

Kindness is a language which the deaf can hear and the blind can see. *(Mark Twain)* What will my behaviors, words, and interactions speak to others today?

PRAYER

God of Love, lead us in Your ways of kindness and understanding as we serve with our co-workers and bring healing to those who come into our care each day. May our touch, our words, and our manner of relating reflect Your goodness. Amen

March 25

REFLECTION

I am the handmaid of the Lord. May it be done to me according to your word. And the Word became flesh and made his dwelling among us. *(Luke 1:38; John 1:14)* In what ways may God be asking to become flesh and dwell within me today?

PRAYER

Ever-Present God, make us more aware of the wonder and mystery of how You invite us each day to carry Your presence within us. May all that You desire to happen in and through us, be done according to Your Word. Amen

March 26

REFLECTION

You changed my mourning into dancing; O Lord, my God, forever will I give you thanks. *(Psalm 30:12a,13b)* Has there been a time in my life when I experienced darkness, sadness, or uncertainty? When and how did God give me comfort and lead me through this time?

PRAYER

God of Comfort, thank You for the ways You continue to reveal Your presence and care in my life and in the lives of those I love and care for. Help us to rely on You with faith and hope when darkness, uncertainty, or pain come to us. Amen

March 27

REFLECTION

I will prove my holiness through you. I will pour clean water upon you. I will give you a new spirit. *(Ezekiel 36:23-26)* How have I experienced God renewing and refreshing me in this Season of Lent as we prepare to celebrate Easter?

PRAYER

Renewing God, refresh my spirit as we move toward the celebration of Easter. In Your mercy and compassion, create a clean and generous heart within me. Amen

March 28

REFLECTION

If you remain in my word, you will truly be my disciple. You will know the truth, and the truth will set you free. *(John 8:31-32)* Perhaps some of the deepest truths involve knowing how to love our neighbor, how to forgive those who have hurt us, and how to be open to God's guidance in our lives. How do I seek these deeper truths in my life?

PRAYER

God of Truth, guide and direct us each day that we may know Your word and grow to be Your disciples as we walk the path before us. Show us how to seek Your deeper truths that we may grow in wisdom and grace. Amen

March 29

REFLECTION

The one who sent me is with me. He has not left me alone, because I always do what is pleasing to him. *(John 8:29)* As I go about the hours and events of my day, do I sense that God is with me and I am not alone? How do I know that my life and actions are pleasing to God?

PRAYER

God-with-us, thank You for Your abiding presence within and around us. As we serve others and interact with our co-workers and families, guide our actions so that all we do is pleasing to You and serves the common good. Amen

March 30
A Prayer for Doctors

REFLECTION

Today let us honor and give thanks to God for all physicians who serve as part of our local healthcare services and for all people whom they serve. We ask God to renew within all physicians their own personal experience of being called to bring healing and comfort to those who are injured and ill.

PRAYER

Gracious God, we thank you today for the skill, leadership, care and compassion of all physicians, especially those who serve among us in our local healthcare systems. Guide and bless the work of their hands, their minds and hearts as they diagnose, treat and comfort all those in need. Amen

March 31

REFLECTION

At times, it seems that our society would like us to think that life is about being always successful, young, and independent. Yet with life experience, we come to learn that it is more about being vulnerable, broken, caring, loving, responsible, and interdependent. What wisdom have I learned from the times in life when I felt vulnerable or broken?

PRAYER

Creator God, thank You for the times in our lives when we have felt vulnerable, humbled, or broken. Teach us to use these experiences to grow in understanding, compassion and wisdom. Amen

April

April 1

REFLECTION

We may find that when we forgive or heal others, we also heal ourselves. In learning and acting with compassion, we become more ourselves, more whole, more fully human. How might I be called to extend forgiveness or a healing touch today?

PRAYER

God of Mercy, show us how to bring compassion and healing in the midst of suffering and pain. Open our eyes that we may see You in the sick and injured persons who come to us in need. Amen

April 2

REFLECTION

Hope is patience with a lamp lit. *(Tertullian)* What helps to kindle the lamp of patience and hope in my life?

PRAYER

God of Hope, teach us how to maintain an attitude and perspective of patience as we meet the unexpected or uncertain events and situations in our lives. May the lamp of Your light and Your truth guide our path in all we do. Amen

April 3

REFLECTION

You were once darkness, but now you are light in the Lord. Live as children of light, for light produces every kind of goodness and righteousness and truth. Try to learn what is pleasing to the Lord. *(Ephesians 5:8-10)* Do my life and my actions bring light and goodness to those I meet each day?

PRAYER

God of Light, continue to guide us to walk in Your ways so that Your goodness and truth may shine in our lives. In the quiet of our hearts and in our interactions with others may we learn each day what is pleasing to You. Amen

April 4

REFLECTION

In the Gospel, when some of the disciples had been fishing all night and caught nothing, Jesus told them to put their nets out into deeper water and possibly even in a different direction. When they did this, they had a very pleasant surprise. *(Luke 5:1-11)* When I am feeling frustrated, tired, or empty, what does God often guide me to do?

PRAYER

Faithful God, when we are feeling frustrated, tired, or empty, we trust that You are with us and will see us through. Quiet our minds and hearts so that we might hear Your voice and follow in Your ways. Amen.

April 5

REFLECTION

In the Gospels, Jesus is often responding to a request of a person in need of healing, or from a relative of the person in need. He reaches out to touch them or they reach out to him. What a privilege and an honor we have to continue the healing ministry of Jesus in our healthcare setting. How will I offer the healing touch of God today?

PRAYER

Compassionate God, guide our hands and our work that we may be instruments of Your healing care, Your healing touch for all we meet each day. Thank You for this ministry which You entrust to each of us. Amen

April 6

REFLECTION

If your actions inspire others to dream more, learn more, do more, you are a leader. *(John Quincy Adams)* Do my actions and interactions with others inspire and encourage them in any way?

PRAYER

Life-giving God, thank You for friends, family members, and co-workers who inspire and encourage us to be and to do all we can as we live and work together. Give us a positive and generous spirit as we serve others in Your name. Amen

April 7

REFLECTION

Although the world is full of suffering, it is full also of the overcoming of it. *(Helen Keller)* As I experience suffering in my own life and in the lives of others, what can I do to ease the pain and share the compassion which gives comfort?

Ever-present God, as we experience the suffering and struggles of life, we trust that You are with us giving courage and strength to see us through. Thank You for the people whose lives witness the resiliency of the human spirit and who share compassion with all those in need. Amen

April 8

REFLECTION

Alleluia! Jesus is risen and lives among us! How do I experience the miracle of resurrection and new life today? How can I share this hope and promise with others as we celebrate the mystery and wonder of this gift?

PRAYER

Risen Jesus, help us to recognize You present in our lives today. Lead us from darkness to light, that we may share gifts of hope and new life with those we encounter each day. Amen

April 9

REFLECTION

The Easter story gives life to our deepest hope – our hope in God's power to bring life out of suffering and death. There is a power greater than our own – God can bring new life to all persons and all things. How will I let God bring new life to me in this Easter season?

PRAYER

Amazing God, You turn our fear into joy. You bring new life from suffering and death. Touch our lives with Easter hope, so that we may share the power and goodness of Your love with those we serve and work among. Amen

April 10

REFLECTION

To do Your will is my delight; my God, Your law is in my heart. *(Psalm 40:9)* How will my "yes" invite God to live and work in and through me today?

PRAYER

Loving God, help me to find delight and joy in embracing Your law and Your ways in my heart and in my life as I seek to serve others today. Help me to say "yes" to You in the times of tiredness as well as in the times of joy. Amen

April 11

REFLECTION

You will show me the path of life and fullness of joy in Your presence. *(Psalm 16:11)* When do I know that I am walking the "path of life" which God desires for me?

PRAYER

Loving and Faithful God, guide me along the path I should walk today. Knowing that You are leading the way will bring joy and satisfaction in all I do, as I seek to serve You and Your people in need this day. Amen

April 12

REFLECTION

Let the children come to me, and do not stop them. To such as these belongs the Kingdom of God. *(Mark 10:14)* Who are the children that may need my special care and attention today?

PRAYER

Life-giving God, help me to be aware of all the children I will meet along the way today… the children I see in the halls, with parents and grandparents; the sick or injured children brought to us for care; children who are happy and free; children who are afraid and anxious. Help us welcome and care for them with gentleness and tender hearts. Amen

April 13

REFLECTION

Take time to quiet your mind and remember to dream. Feel the energy greater than yourself that dwells within and around you. See the spring colors as brightly as they are meant to be seen. Breathe in the freshness of life which sometimes escapes us when our lives become too busy.

PRAYER

Ever-present God, even in the business of this day, help me to slow down to "smell the flowers" and breathe in the colors and freshness of this wonderful Spring Season with which You have blessed us. Refresh my mind and heart so that my life expresses gratitude to You each day, Amen

April 14

REFLECTION

Reach out for the hand that has been waiting for your grasp. Touch life again as if for the first time with all your heart. We can lose days by not seeing what is already there – the spiritual enlightenment that awakens our soul. In what ways do I need to be awakened to the beauty of life and persons around me today?

PRAYER

Awakening God, reach out to touch and awaken me today. Open my eyes and my heart to the spiritual enlightenment which I may otherwise miss as I quickly rush through my day and all it calls me to do. Amen

April 15

REFLECTION

I have seen the Lord! *(John 20:18)* Those who saw and spoke with Jesus after His resurrection were filled with awe, excitement, and sometimes disbelief at first. Jesus is still very much present and with us every day. How might He reveal His presence to me today? When will I hear His voice or see His face among us?

PRAYER

God-with-us, soften our hearts, open our eyes, and attune our ears to recognize Your presence, Your voice, Your face among us today. You so often come to us in ordinary and unexpected ways. Help us not to miss You as You come to walk among us. Amen

April 16

REFLECTION

Be on the lookout for God's blessings and mercies. The more we look for them, the more we will see them. How will God's blessings surprise and give joy to me today?

PRAYER

Merciful and Good God, open our eyes and our awareness to recognize and give thanks for Your blessings which come to us each day. Help us to see You present and acting in the ordinary events of our lives. Amen

April 17

REFLECTION

We are called to bless, affirm, and encourage each other on our faith journey. Who may need to hear a good word from me today?

PRAYER

Eternal God, as we walk the journey of life with You and with one another, show us ways of affirming and encouraging each other. Help us be attentive to those in need around us each day, for we may not know the burden they carry. Amen

April 18

REFLECTION

We may find that what we possess comes to have double the value when we take the opportunity to share it with others. What might others need me to share with them today… a kind word, a smile, a helping hand, a healing touch?

PRAYER

Gracious God, make us ever aware of Your abundant blessings showered upon each of us. Let us find joy in sharing what we have to encourage or lighten the load of those we meet today. Amen

April 19

REFLECTION

It is best to refrain from judging the lives of others, because each person knows only their own pain and their own journey. It's one thing to feel that you are on the right path, but it's another to think that yours is the only path. How will I open myself to more fully understand and appreciate others today?

PRAYER

Ever-Present God, guide my heart and my path each day. Help me to be faithful to Your direction and not just to my own desires or needs. Give me a discerning spirit to recognize these when they differ. Guide me to appreciate and respect all those I encounter each day. Amen

April 20

REFLECTION

How do we know if we have patience, unless we have needed to wait many times for things to happen which are not in our control? How do we know if we have strength and courage unless we have suffered?

PRAYER

Sustaining God, give us patience, strength and courage as we walk our paths in life. Help us to learn and to grow in the events of life which call for patience and in our times of suffering. Amen

April 21

REFLECTION

Washing one another's feet means, above all, tirelessly forgiving one another, beginning together ever anew. *(Benedict XVI)* How might I be called to "wash the feet" of another person today?

PRAYER

Forgiving God, give us humble hearts and attitudes as we interact with our co-workers, our family, and those we are called to serve today. Teach us how to "wash the feet" of those You place in our lives each day. Amen

April 22

REFLECTION

Were not our hearts burning within us as he spoke to us on the road… and when we came to know him in the breaking of the bread? *(John 24:32,35)* When might I meet Jesus this week as I walk the journey of life or as I share a meal with another person?

PRAYER

God of Surprises, open our eyes and inner awareness that we may recognize and welcome You as You enter our lives, walk with us, or share a meal with us. Your image and likeness dwells in each person. Help us to honor and reverence all those we meet today. Amen

April 23

REFLECTION

When Jesus overcame death, it was so that we can do the same through him. His life, his death, and his resurrection are what made it possible for all of us to have eternal life. It what ways do I live and share this hope and promise?

PRAYER

God of Hope and New Life, the joy of Christ's resurrection fills the whole earth. May it also bring hope and joy to all of us as we celebrate this miracle and wonder of eternal life. Amen

April 24

REFLECTION

A key characteristic of the people of God is that they care for those in need. Who around me most needs my help today … a patient, a visitor, a co-worker, a physician, a family member, a person on the phone?

PRAYER

Caring God, help me to notice today those who are most in need of my kindness and generosity. Then guide me to give with unconditional love as You have given to me. Amen

April 25

REFLECTION

When we experience illness, injuries and loss in our lives, we are faced with a choice of whether these will make us a bitter person or better person. After the initial shock and sadness of these experiences, which choice do I usually strive to make?

PRAYER

Life-giving God, as we experience illness, injury and loss in our lives, we find how precious yet fragile life truly is. Guide and strengthen us to find in these experiences ways to become wounded healers, and to discover the deeper meaning and beauty in life. Amen

April 26

REFLECTION

The sun dawned this morning as I have never seen it before; it seems I have never seen it shine as it has today. It was more than shining, it seemed to be glowing and pulsing with life. What gifts of light and nature have been transforming me in this lovely Spring Season?

PRAYER

Life-giving God, open my awareness and my senses to notice and give thanks for the gifts and blessings of this new day. May Your light and Your presence transform all of life within me and around me today as I seek to serve others in Your name. Amen

April 27

REFLECTION

Ever since God revealed the divine name to Moses *(Exodus 6:1-4)*, people of faith have been discovering that God's "I AM" is well translated as *I am for you, I am with you.* How do I experience God *for me* and *with me* in my life?

PRAYER

Ever-Present God, help me to take quiet moments aside in my day to recognize and give thanks for all the ways You are truly for us and with us. In my brokenness, give me strength and wisdom. Amen

April 28

REFLECTION

Often in our lives, the most precious and cherished gift of love we share with another is spelled T-I-M-E. Who might be in most need of my gift of love, presence, and compassion this week?

God of Love, You are always present to us as we turn to You and even when we fail to acknowledge You. Guide us to share with others what is most important and precious to them today. Help us to keep our focus and priorities set on the greater good which You reveal to us. Amen

April 29

REFLECTION

After his resurrection, Jesus came to be with his disciples. He said, "Peace be with you", and showed them the wounds in his body. *(John 20:19-20)* As we are recovering from the hurts and wounds which life brings, are we able to bring peace, hope, or forgiveness to others? If not, what do we bring?

PRAYER

Wounded and Risen Lord, teach us how to embrace the wounds and hurts which life brings. Let Your gift of Peace fill our lives when we are hurt or discouraged. Free us so that we may bring peace, hope, and forgiveness to others. Amen

April 30

REFLECTION

In the Gospel of John after the resurrection of Jesus, the disciples had fished all night but caught nothing. At dawn Jesus appeared to them and asked how the fishing had been. He then told them to cast their net out again and their net was filled to overflowing. *(John 21:1-14)* When we have labored long and hard, yet things still don't seem to go as we had planned, what do we do? Who do we turn to for help?

PRAYER

Faithful God, deepen our trust in You as we face the difficulties and disappointments of life. Please answer our prayers in the times and ways which You know are best for all concerned. Amen

May

May 1

REFLECTION

Those who listen well are often the best teachers and mentors. They teach by their example, their kindness and understanding. When they speak, they often have something worthwhile to say from the inner wisdom they have gained. How well do I listen? Is my mind often formulating what I will say next or truly still and open enough to listen?

PRAYER

Listening God, You are attentive to us in every way as we go about our day. You know our needs and deepest desires even before we speak them. Teach us the wisdom and compassion of Your listening presence as we interact with others each day. Amen

May 2

REFLECTION

When we forgive others, we also free ourselves. When we don't forgive, we keep ourselves held bound. When we forgive, we don't have to become best friends. We do need to give up trying to hurt in return or else we are not free. How am I with letting go and forgiving others in my life?

PRAYER

God of Easter Peace, teach us Your ways of forgiving and letting go. Free our hearts, our minds, our spirits of the poison of revenge or hurting in return. Fill us with Your Peace and New Life. Amen

May 3

REFLECTION

Science can give us knowledge. Spirituality can give us meaning and wisdom. We need both for a full and healthy existence. When have I felt a sense of wholeness and harmony in my life? What led me to this experience?

PRAYER

God of Wisdom, guide us in our lives and ministry to use the knowledge and skill we learn from science, as well as the deeper meaning and wisdom we gain from Your Spirit within us, to bring healing and wellness to those we serve. Amen

May 4

REFLECTION

There is enough in the world to fill our basic needs, but not for all our greed. *(Mother Teresa of Calcutta)* How do I distinguish my needs from my greed?

PRAYER

Providential God, through all of Your creation and the work of our hands, You daily provide for us. Teach us how to live simply, so that others may simply live. Help us to reflect and distinguish between what is our need and what is our greed. Amen

May 5
A Prayer for Nurses

Gracious God, bless our nurses whom you have chosen to be instruments of your healing. Anoint them to be humble and skilled servants of your grace. Where there is danger, may they protect life; where there is weakness and pain, may they provide relief and comfort; where there is anxiety and fear, may they offer gentle reassurances through their presence and kindness; and in the times when all human efforts fail, may they rest assured that those they have cared for will live forever with you. Bless all nurses with a gentle and compassionate heart, that they may be channels of your healing touch each day. Amen

May 6

REFLECTION

Clothe yourselves with humility in your dealings with one another, for God's favor rests on the humble, not on the proud. *(1 Peter 5:5)* What do I display in my dealings with others around me? Do I relate in a spirit of humility?

PRAYER

God of Truth, create in us a humble spirit and a servant's heart as we interact with others and serve Your people in need of healing and kindness. Help us to act out of love and not in judgment when our human minds do not understand. Amen

May 7

REFLECTION

It's the nature of our soul that often determines how we make our journey in life, not necessarily the calm or the strife which life presents. What is the nature of my soul? How do I nurture my soul for wholeness and health?

PRAYER

Life-giving God, help us to be attentive to the nature of our soul… that eternal inner spirit which You have breathed into each of us. Guide us in ways which help us to renew our souls for wholeness and health as we serve Your people in need. Amen

May 8

REFLECTION

What women in your life have nurtured and given life to you… your mother, grandmother, aunt, sister, mentor, friend? Whether they are living now or have already gone before us, take time today to thank them and rejoice in their goodness.

PRAYER

God of Life, thank You for our mothers, grandmothers, and other women who have given us life and continue to nurture life within us. Bless all those we love with strong faith and good health, as we rejoice in Your gift of life today. Amen

May 9

REFLECTION

With God, nothing will be impossible. *(Luke 1:37)* In the midst of our busy schedules, troubles, concerns, and worries, do we leave any room for God's actions and miracles?

PRAYER

Ever-Present God, as we go about our day, nudge us to be aware of Your signs and wonders among us. With You as our Faithful Companion, nothing is impossible. Amen

May 10

REFLECTION

God has put something noble and good in every person. When I look at others do I usually focus on the good or on their perceived flaws?

PRAYER

God our Creator, thank You for the noble and the good which You have placed within each person You have made. As we interact with each other, and experience our humanness and brokenness, help us to look deeper to see the positive and the glowing goodness as well. Amen

May 11

REFLECTION

Cheerfulness is among the most contagious virtues. It blesses those who practice it and those who experience it. Do others experience a genuine uplifting cheerfulness in my attitude and behavior?

PRAYER

Life-Giving God, touch our hearts and our spirits each day with delight and joy in the gift of life You have given us. May our behaviors and attitudes bring hope and healing to all we serve. Amen

May 12

REFLECTION

It's the simple things in life that most often make living worthwhile… kindness, patience, a pleasant word, a welcoming smile, gratitude and appreciation. What are the simple things in life which motivate and give meaning to my life each day?

PRAYER

Eternal God, lead us to find joy and contentment in the simple things in life…each one a special gift from You. Help us to be aware that the small kindnesses we offer to others may give hope and meaning to their life in the midst of suffering, anxiety, or loss. Amen

May 13

REFLECTION

Be full of empathy and kindness toward each other; care for one another with tender hearts and humble spirits. What do others experience in my interactions with them each day? Do my attitudes and behaviors lift up or drag down?

PRAYER

All Knowing God, You see and understand the joys and the struggles that each of us encounter each day. Awaken us to grow in patience and understanding. Give us tender hearts and humble spirits as we live and serve each day. Amen

May 14

REFLECTION

Do you know any farmers or gardeners who grow fresh vegetables and fruit for our enjoyment? Let us ask God's blessings upon them today in the midst of this planting and growing season.

PRAYER

Loving God, Creator of the Earth, we pray today for all farmers and gardeners in this planting and growing season. Bless and provide for them in all of their needs. May the work they do bring forth an abundant harvest to help feed the people of our country and our world. Amen

May 15

REFLECTION

The Lord is my Shepherd, there is nothing I shall want; beside restful waters he leads me, he refreshes my soul. *(Psalm 23)* In what ways do I look to God to be my Shepherd and guide in life? When and how do I recognize God's voice and call in my life?

PRAYER

Good and Caring Shepherd, thank You for the ways You lead and guide me along my journey in life. Lead me to quiet moments and places where I can hear Your voice and be refreshed in body and spirit as I seek to serve in Your name. Amen

May 16

REFLECTION

Wherever there is a human being, there is an opportunity for a kindness. Kind words can be short and easy to speak, but their echoes are truly endless. *(Mother Theresa of Calcutta)* What opportunities for kindness will I have today? How will I respond?

PRAYER

God of endless opportunities, guide me today that I may see the persons who need kindness and kind words spoken to them. Let all that I do be a reflection and echo of Your love and goodness for all those I encounter each day. Amen

May 17

REFLECTION

The wonderful diverse gifts of God's Holy Spirit to individuals do not compete with each other, but are meant to create an experience of community in peace, appreciation, and service to all in need. How am I with appreciating and using the gifts and skills I have been given and appreciating those of my co-workers as well?

PRAYER

Holy Spirit of God, thank You for the wonderful variety of gifts given to each of us individually and as a faith community. Guide each of us to use and appreciate what we have been given and also recognize and support the gifts shared by those we work and live among. Amen

May 18

REFLECTION

Give generously from the best of who you are. The more you give from your heart's treasures, the more God will multiply for you and for those with whom you share. As I share the best of who I am and what I have, how have I seen God blessing me and others in abundant ways?

PRAYER

Life-Giving God, open our hearts to share the best of who we are and the gifts we have been given. May our lives and our service reveal the abundance of Your goodness and generosity among us. Amen

May 19

REFLECTION

One of the key messages we read in the Scriptures and sacred writings is that God is faithful and will not abandon us. How have I experienced God's faithfulness, love and care as I walk the journey of life, especially in times of struggle or darkness?

PRAYER

Faithful God, open my eyes and my spirit to recognize all the ways You are present and provide for me along life's journey. In times of struggle or darkness, increase my trust to know You are with me and will see me through whatever may come. Amen

May 20

REFLECTION

For forty days after his resurrection, Jesus continued to appear to his disciples to reassure them and to encourage them. When he ascended to heaven, he told them they would receive power and special gifts when his Holy Spirit came upon them. *(Acts 1:1-11)* What gifts do I feel I have been given to serve, to bring life and encouragement to others as I live and pray each day?

PRAYER

Eternal and Living God, thank You for empowering and blessing each of us with gifts for bringing life and encouragement to those we live among and serve. May all we do reflect Your goodness and serve the common good. Amen

May 21

REFLECTION

My friend shall forever be my friend, and reflect a ray of God for me. *(Henry David Thoreau)* Who reflects the light and goodness of God to me?

PRAYER

God-with-us, thank You for those who reflect Your light and goodness to me, those who are true and faithful friends. Touch my life that I may also reflect Your light and goodness in unselfish and generous ways. Amen

May 22

REFLECTION

Never lose an opportunity of seeing anything that is beautiful. Welcome it in every face, in every sky, in every flower. *(Ralph Waldo Emerson)* What will I take time to gaze upon that is beautiful today? Stop to cherish each opportunity.

PRAYER

God of Beauty and Wonder, in the moments of this day, nudge me to pause and delight in the moments of beauty You will place in my path. May the simple beauties I discover in this day refresh my spirit. Amen

May 23

REFLECTION

When crossing a river, remove your sandals. When crossing a border, remove your crown. *(Southeast Asian Proverb)* What might I need to remove from my head, judgment or attitude in order to relate in a more humble and understanding way with a patient, family member, or co-worker?

PRAYER

God of Wisdom, guide us to know what it is we may need to remove within ourselves in order to relate well with those we serve and work among each day. Guide us to live in truth and humility. Remove any arrogance within us. Amen

May 24

REFLECTION

The whole caring and healing consciousness is contained within each single caring moment. How conscious am I that each moment of showing care in my day has the potential to bring healing at some level to another person?

PRAYER

Healing God, make us more aware during our daily tasks and routines that each moment in our day holds the potential to bring caring and healing to others. Guide and direct us in our caring behaviors and attitudes each day. Amen

May 25

REFLECTION

I am only one; but I am still one. I cannot do everything, but I can do something. I will not refuse to do the something I am able to do. *(Helen Keller)* Whether it may seem small or big at this time, what opportunities will I have today to use my gifts, skills and talents to make a difference in someone's life?

PRAYER

Life-Giving God, keep our minds and hearts open to recognize the moments in our day when we are called to make a difference by using our skills and talents for the good of someone we are called to serve, assist or encourage. Amen

May 26

REFLECTION

The two Great Commandments are these: You shall love the Lord your God with all your heart, with all your soul, with all your mind, and with all your strength. You shall love your neighbor as yourself. *(Mark 12:29-31)* Which of these is most challenging to me at this time?

PRAYER

Creator God, the loving relationships You call us to embrace and grow in are simply stated, yet can be very challenging at times. Help us to see as You see, understand as You understand, and love as You love. Amen

May 27

REFLECTION

We learn in the Scriptures of Pentecost that the strength of our unity allows us to embrace the rich diversity among us. The fruits of the Spirit in our lives are love, joy, peace, patience, kindness, generosity, faithfulness, gentleness, and self-control. *(Galatians 5:22-23)* Which of these are most evident in my life? Which ones need nurturing or renewing within me?

PRAYER

Holy Spirit of God, rest upon us again this day. Renew us, guide us, transform us so that the fruits of Your presence may be alive and evident in our lives. Strengthen the unity among us as we embrace the diversity of gifts and skills shared for our ministry of healing and compassion. Amen

May 28

REFLECTION

Positive energy is inspiring, life-giving, and contagious. What kind of energy do I bring to my work and to my relationships? What do others feel from me as I interact with them each day?

PRAYER

Ever-Present God, bless each of us with a life-giving positive energy which inspires, lifts up and encourages those we are called to serve and work among. Help us to have the vision to see new possibilities in the midst of what might initially seem hopeless or impossible. Amen

May 29

REFLECTION

Through the ages, within many faith traditions and sacred writings, God has been revealed through many metaphors, stories, and names. Along your journey of life and now in the present, what stories and names for God have been most significant to you? How do you name and speak to God as you pray?

PRAYER

Amazing God, our knowledge and awareness of who You are is still so limited and beyond our understanding. Thank You for the surprising and beautiful ways You continue to reveal Yourself to us as we journey through life. We treasure the experiences, stories and names which help us to recognize Your action and presence in our lives. Amen

May 30

REFLECTION

Today let us remember and honor those gone before us who have served our country, our families, and our faith communities. We hold them with special reverence as we give thanks to God for their lives, their witness, the love and gifts of freedom they have shared with each of us.

PRAYER

Gracious God, we give thanks for those gone before us who have served their country, their families, their communities in self-less and generous ways. We pray that they may now be enjoying the fullness of peace and joy with You for all eternity. Amen

May 31

REFLECTION

Blessed be our God of compassion and all encouragement, who encourages us in every affliction, so that we may be able to encourage others in their times of affliction, with the encouragement we ourselves have received. *(2 Corinthians 1:3-4)* When have I felt God's comfort, compassion, and encouragement in my life? In what ways do I pass this on to others in their time of need?

PRAYER

God of Compassion, thank You for the times You have reached out to me directly or through others to give comfort and encouragement in my times of pain or struggle. Guide me to share these same gifts with others in their own times of struggle. Amen

June

June 1

REFLECTION

Let your light shine before others, that they may see your good deeds and give glory to God. *(Matthew 5:16)* What is the light and goodness that God has placed within me to shine and share with others? How well do I let it shine for God's glory?

PRAYER

Life-Giving God, thank You for the light and goodness You have created within me and all those I live and interact with each day. Help us to always rejoice in Your light and give thanks for Your presence and goodness among us. Amen

June 2

REFLECTION

Knowing what to say is not always necessary; just the presence of a caring person can make a world of difference. How do my actions, attitudes, and behaviors bring a caring presence to those around me?

PRAYER

Ever-Present God, teach us the power and gift of a true caring presence, as we attend to those who come to us for healing and as we serve with one another. Amen

June 3

REFLECTION

Laughter is a medicine for life; being able to laugh at oneself can often bring healing. What makes me uptight or somber in my life? Do I open my heart and my spirit to the healing power of laughter and humor?

PRAYER

Healing God, open us to welcome the gifts of laughter and humor in our lives. Nudge us when we are taking ourselves or life too seriously. Show us how to encourage the hearts and lift the spirits of those around us with the medicine of good humor and laughter. Amen

June 4

REFLECTION

We hold this treasure in earthen vessels, that the surpassing power may be of God and not from us. *(2 Corinthians 4:7)* How do I experience the "earthen vessel" of my life as holding the special gifts and power of God to be given for others?

PRAYER

Indwelling God, thank You for Your presence and power living within us as individuals and as a faith community. Give us the humility to recognize the clay vessels we are, yet also let Your light and gifts be shared in our lives. Amen

June 5

REFLECTION

I speak this while I am still with them so that they may share my joy completely. *(John 17:13)* What special joy have I experienced recently?

PRAYER

God of Peace and Joy, thank You for the times You delight our hearts through the small and ordinary experiences in life. Create in us an open and child-like spirit to notice and share these joys as wondrous gifts from You. Amen

June 6

REFLECTION

In the Hebrew Scriptures we read, "an eye for an eye, a tooth for a tooth" is the way to relate when serious injury happens. *(Exodus 21:24)* In the Christian Scriptures, Jesus calls us to another way of relating… do not strike back, go the extra mile, give to the one in need, and do not pass on hurt or evil. *(Matthew 5:38-42)* How do I usually respond when someone hurts me or those I love?

PRAYER

Loving God, how challenging Your call can be at various times in our lives. Give us largeness of heart, strength, wisdom, and courage to relate in healthy and good ways with all persons we meet each day. Amen

June 7

REFLECTION

I say to you, love your enemies, and pray for those who persecute you. *(Matthew 5:44)* Could there be anything in life much more challenging that this? How can I find the strength, courage, and love to do this?

PRAYER

God of Challenges, when we feel hurt, rejected, betrayed, dismissed, and in pain, You ask us to somehow love and pray for those who have wronged us. This can feel beyond our ability and maybe even feel impossible at times. Guide us with Your strength to at least begin to pray for the desire to forgive and to love. Walk with us on our journey each day. Amen

June 8

REFLECTION

Whoever sows sparingly will also reap sparingly, and whoever sows abundantly will also reap abundantly. *(2 Corinthians 9:6)* How generously do I sow kindness, encouragement, and understanding for others each day?

PRAYER

Amazing God, show me how to live and share goodness with others in abundance and with a generous spirit each day. Open my eyes to see the constant blessings You give to me every day that I may live with a spirit of gratitude. Amen

June 9

REFLECTION

Have you observed that the more anger or hurt we carry from the past in our hearts, the less capable we are of loving fully in the present? What do I do to help free myself of anger and past hurts in my life, so that I do not pass on hurt or pain to others?

PRAYER

Liberating God, give me insight, wisdom, and courage to know how to let You free my heart of any anger, resentment, or hurt I may be carrying within me. Refresh my spirit and vision to love more fully in each new day. Amen

June 10

REFLECTION

Part of the virtue of courage is discovering that you may not win, yet you keep trying anyway. When in my life have I kept on trying even when things were uncertain, outcomes unknown, yet hope kept me on the journey?

PRAYER

Faithful God, continue to guide and sustain us along life's journey especially in times of uncertainty and when outcomes are unknown. Help us to see that being faithful to the efforts and the journey with courage and hope is a victory in itself. Amen

June 11

REFLECTION

One sign of knowing when you're at your best is when you're focused, serious and passionate about what you do, but at the same time you can relax, have fun and feel confident. How do I know when I am at my best in my work and in my relationships?

PRAYER

God our Creator, guide us to be the best we can be each day in what we do at work and also in our relationships with You, our families, our co-workers. May Your light and the gifts, talents, skills You have blessed us with be shared in all we do. Amen

June 12

REFLECTION

A person of care and compassion strives to understand the situation or pain of another as it affects the other's life; seeks to understand the other person's perspective; avoids making assumptions; seeks to understand the other's experience. How well do I truly listen, seek to understand, and avoid making assumptions in my interactions with others?

Faithful God, soften my heart to know and offer true compassion, avoid quick judgments and assumptions. Help me to have the ability to understand and reverence the perspective and experience of those I serve and work among. Amen

June 13

REFLECTION

Attribute to God every good that you have received. Otherwise you are taking credit for something that does not truly belong to you. *(St. Anthony of Padua)* What blessings have I received from God which I give thanks for every day or often?

PRAYER

Eternal Providing God, thank You for every good which we receive from You each day. Help us to live from a spirit of gratitude; to live with open hands receiving and sharing our blessings with others throughout our lives. Amen

June 14

REFLECTION

Those who do justice will live in the presence of the Lord. In the Hebrew Scriptures, to "do justice" is to live in right relationship with God, with other persons, and with all God's creation. How will I live in and do "justice" today?

PRAYER

God of Justice, guide my path today that I might live in right relationship with You, with co-workers, family members, and all those I am called to serve. May all I do reflect Your compassion and goodness. Amen

June 15

REFLECTION

Let your light shine today. Someone along the path in your day may need just the gift and quality of light which your life will give. How will the gift of light, kindness, care or compassion shine in me today?

PRAYER

Eternal God, guide me in Your ways so that the light of hope, goodness, comfort and healing with shine forth from me for those who may need it at this time in their life. Amen

June 16

REFLECTION

Things turn out best for the people who make the best of the way things turn out. How will I respond today in the midst of unexpected interruptions or unanticipated outcomes?

PRAYER

Merciful and Forgiving God, give us patience, and a sense of flexibility and understanding as we encounter the events of our day and the persons who come into our lives. Guide us to make the best of each situation for the good of all concerned. Amen

June 17

REFLECTION

A leper approached Jesus and said, "Lord, if you wish, you can make me clean." Jesus stretched out his hand, touched the man, and said, "I do wish this. Be made clean." With this, the man's leprosy was cleansed. *(Matthew 8:2-3)* What opportunities might God give me today to be an agent of healing for another person in need?

PRAYER

Healing God, thank You for inviting and calling us to be a part of Your healing ministry. Guide our minds and our hands that we will use the gifts, skills, and abilities You have given to each of us for healing and caring for those in need. Amen

June 18

REFLECTION

Like Sarah, in the Hebrew Scriptures, we may sometimes laugh and find great joy welling up within us because what God is doing in our lives seems so unexpected and surprising. *(Genesis 18:1-15)* What have you experienced recently in your life as a surprise from God which brings you joy or delight?

PRAYER

God of Surprises, open my eyes and my spirit to see and delight in the new and surprising ways You enter our lives to lift us up and bring us joy. Guide us to live with hearts full of gratitude and trust in Your loving care. Amen

June 19

REFLECTION

Who are the men in your life who have modeled what it is to be a good father, grandfather, husband, brother, mentor in life? What qualities, virtues, and strengths do they have and share with others?

PRAYER

Loving God, thank You today for our fathers, grandfathers and husbands, both living and deceased. Thank you for the blessing they have been and continue to be in our lives. Bless each of them today with what they need to serve their families and model the goodness which reflects Your presence among us. Amen

June 20

If the only tool you have is a hammer, you tend to see every problem as a nail. *(Abraham Maslow)* Tenderness and kindness are not signs of weakness, but manifestations of strength and resolution. *(Khalil Gibran)* What "tools" do I carry in my mind, heart, and hands as I work and serve with others each day?

PRAYER

God of Tender Mercies, free us of any harshness and judgmental ways which still dwell within our hearts. May the strength and resolve we share with others be shown by the tenderness and kindness in our actions and words. Amen

June 21

REFLECTION

Prayer does not change God, it changes the one who prays. When I pray, how do I pray and what do I usually pray for? What does "give us this day our daily bread" and "Thy will be done" mean to me?

PRAYER

Wise and Gracious God, I pray today that the desires of my heart and the good I wish for others will be answered in the time and in the way that You know is best for each of us. May Your will be done in our lives. Amen

June 22

REFLECTION

We are God's handiwork, created in Christ Jesus for the good works that God has prepared. *(Ephesians 2:10)* What good works of kindness, compassion, mercy, healing might God desire to give through me today?

PRAYER

Life-Giving God, You create us in Your own image and invite us to reflect Your love and goodness in our lives each day. Direct our hearts and our actions so that those we serve and interact with may experience Your providential care. Amen

June 23

REFLECTION

Be merciful, as your Father is merciful. Do not judge and you will not be judged. Do not condemn and you will not be condemned. Forgive and you will be forgiven. Give and gifts will be given to you in good measure, packed together, shaken down and overflowing. For the measure with which you measure will in return be measured out to you. *(Luke 6:36-3)* Look for the times and the ways that God may call you today to offer a good measure of understanding, forgiveness, or mercy to others.

PRAYER

God of Mercy, soften our hearts so that we can refrain from judging others. Many persons may come into our care who need the healing which forgiveness, encouragement, and kindness can bring. Use each of us as Your instruments for this healing today. Amen

June 24

REFLECTION

You would not exist if you did not have something to bring to the table of life. What are the gifts, talents, purpose of my life which I am called to bring to the "table of life" and share for the common good?

PRAYER

God, our Creator, You have brought each of us into existence in this time and place in life. Guide us to pause and reflect each day that we may grow in knowing our unique gifts, as well as the purpose and meaning of why You have created us. Amen

June 25

REFLECTION

The greatest discovery of my generation is that a human being can alter his life by altering his attitudes. *(William James)* Is there anything troubling me in my life at this time which I may be able to adjust or change by altering my attitude?

PRAYER

God, Eternal and Ever-New, create in me a new heart, a new mind, a new attitude where life-giving changes need to be made for myself and for the sake of those I live with, work among, and serve. Help my life to bring hope and healing in all I do. Amen

June 26

REFLECTION

In the Gospel of Mark 5:21-43, we read about 3 persons who came to Jesus to ask for healing for ones they loved or for themselves. What they saw in the way Jesus related to people around him gave them trust and confidence to approach him in their time of need and vulnerability. Do others see me as one they can trust and approach in their time of need?

PRAYER

God of Compassion, thank You for welcoming and accepting us as we are, as we come to You in times of need. Guide us to be instruments of Your compassion and healing care for all who come to us as well. Amen

June 27

REFLECTION

In 2 Timothy 4, Paul writes about his life of faith as a meaningful and worthwhile race to be run. All along the way he shares, "The Lord stood by me and gave me strength". How do I experience my journey of life? Do I find it meaningful and worthwhile? Do I experience God with me and giving me strength each day?

PRAYER

Ever-Present God, thank You for the precious gift of life You have given to each of us. Guide us to live with the meaning and purpose You have for our lives as we relate with others and contribute to the common good. Be with us always and sustain us with Your strength. Amen

June 28

REFLECTION

Duty calls us to do things well, but love calls us to do them with true care and compassion. What is my motivation and spirit as I go about my tasks and duties each day?

PRAYER

God our Creator, thank You for the gift of work and the abilities and talents we each have to contribute to the healing ministry in which we serve. Guide and direct our motivations that we may always serve in a spirit of love, care, and compassion. Amen

June 29

REFLECTION

Every thought and feeling we have affects our mental and emotional energy level. The thoughts and feelings we choose to dwell on affect our health and well-being in a positive or negative way. What thoughts and feelings will I choose to dwell on today?

PRAYER

God of Life, guide me today to consciously choose to let my mind and heart be filled with thoughts and feelings which are positive and life-giving for me and for those I serve and work among. Amen

June 30

REFLECTION

Most often happiness doesn't come as a result of getting something we don't have, but rather in recognizing and appreciating what we do have. What tends to bring true happiness and contentment to my life?

PRAYER

Gracious and Generous God, thank You for the blessings You provide for us each day. Touch our hearts to rejoice in our times of abundance and also in our times of having just what we need. Help us always be aware of others' needs as well. Amen

July

July 1

REFLECTION

One important thing in this world is not so much where we stand, but in what direction we are moving. *(Oliver W. Holmes)* What direction does God seem to be leading me in my life? How can I stay aware and faithful on this path?

PRAYER

God of the Journey, guide us along the way that is right and true for our lives, for those we live with and serve. Help us to be faithful on this path and continue to seek direction from You all along the way. Amen

July 2

REFLECTION

The measure with which you measure will be measured out to you. *(Matthew 7:2)* Do I give my best in full measure each day in my work and responsibilities? Do I give of myself in good measure in my relationships with others as well?

PRAYER

Generous God, teach us generosity of heart in all we do. May what we give and do each day flow over in abundance for those we serve and work among. When our day is finished, may we rest well knowing we have given our best in full measure and You will bless us in return. Amen

July 3

REFLECTION

In the Gospel of John 20:24-29, the Apostle Thomas initially experienced doubt about the resurrection and appearance of Jesus to the disciples. For him, "seeing" was believing. Some people see beauty, goodness, and possibility in life because believing helps them to see these. How does this work in my life?

PRAYER

Ever-Present God, in our times of doubt or confusion, open our eyes to see and believe You are with us. Guide us to live each day in hope and in believing so that we may see the beauty, goodness, and endless possibilities in our lives. Amen

July 4
U.S. Independence Day

REFLECTION

We hold these truths to be self-evident, that all men are created equal, that they are endowed by their Creator with certain unalienable Rights, that among these are Life, Liberty and the pursuit of Happiness… And for the support of this Declaration, with a firm reliance on the protection of divine Providence, we mutually pledge to each other our Lives, our Fortunes and our sacred Honor.

(Declaration of Independence July 4, 1776)

PRAYER

Creator God, we thank You today for the freedoms we enjoy in our country because of the courage and wisdom of those who have gone before us and prepared the way. Thank You for guiding the leaders and citizens of our nation who witness to the words of our Declaration of Independence. Let us not take our blessings for granted. Open our hearts to share what we have with persons in need as we embrace the responsibilities which come with our freedoms and blessings. Amen

July 5

REFLECTION

I have learned from experience that the greater part of our happiness or misery depends on our dispositions and not on our circumstances. *(Martha Washington)* With what disposition or attitude do I usually approach life?

PRAYER

Gracious God, guide us to view the circumstances and events of our lives in ways which help us see the possibilities and not just the barriers. Be with us as we walk our journey in life; lift us up and give us hope as we trust in You. Amen

July 6

REFLECTION

I don't know what your destiny will be, but one thing I know: the only ones among you who will be really happy are those who will have sought and found how to serve. *(Albert Schweitzer)* In what ways will I serve and care for others today?

PRAYER

Compassionate God, each day You reach out to be with us and serve our needs. Teach us how to reach out and give in ways which serve the needs of others. Teach us true compassion and care for all we meet each day. Amen

July 7

REFLECTION

For those who believe, no proof is necessary. For those who don't believe, no proof is possible. What do I believe that gives me life, hope, and joy?

PRAYER

Loving God, thank You for believing in each of us, and being our Faithful Friend along life's journey. Deepen our faith in You that we might live each day with trust, hope, and joy in Your presence. Amen

July 8

REFLECTION

In the Scriptures we are called to heal, to cleanse, to set free, and to preach God's Kingdom among us by the way we live our lives. In what specific ways will I be called to do these things today?

PRAYER

Ever Present God, guide us each day that we may have the wisdom, zeal, and compassion to answer Your call and make visible Your Kingdom and Life-giving Presence among us as we live and serve together. Amen

July 9

REFLECTION

Those who trust in God shall understand truth, and the faithful shall abide with God in love; because grace and mercy are with God's holy ones, and God's care is with God's elect. *(Wisdom 3:9)* How do I show my trust and faithfulness in my relationship with God and other persons each day?

PRAYER

God of Wisdom, deepen our trust and faithfulness that we may understand and live in truth and love, serving all Your people with grace and mercy each day. Amen

July 10

REFLECTION

In the Scriptures, Jesus did not send anyone out to travel or serve alone. Even though we may stand alone as we carry out what is ours to do, we need others with us for mutual dialogue, support and encouragement for best results. Who have been faithful and wise companions with me as I have served and walked my journey in life?

PRAYER

Faithful God, You walk the journey of life with us each day as our Companion and Guide. Thank You also for the friends and colleagues who offer wise counsel, support and encouragement as we seek to know and live Your will each day. Amen

July 11

REFLECTION

One of the challenges in life is not just to grow older, but to grow better…to give generously, live realistically, to make our circle of love and care wider, to rejoice and give thanks daily. Am I growing to be a better person as I age and grow each day?

PRAYER

Life-Giving God, thank You for the gift of each new day with the joys, challenges and opportunities it brings. Guide and transform our lives that we may grow to become wiser, kinder, grateful, and more generous in all we do. Amen

July 12

REFLECTION

Have you ever heard the phrase, "nurse a grudge"? What does that really mean if to "nurse" is to seek healing and relieve pain? If you are carrying a grudge, what can you do to help heal it and relieve any anger or resentment which may be draining you?

PRAYER

Healing God, help us to learn how to relate and communicate in a respectful manner with others in our work and in our lives. Guide us to know how to heal hurts, misunderstandings, and not inflict more pain on ourselves or others. Amen

July 13

REFLECTION

God's presence is like the sunshine that warms us, the rain that melts the frost and waters the fields. God's presence is a climate of strong and embracing love, always sustaining and always there. How would I describe the presence of God as I experience it in my life?

PRAYER

Ever-Present God, continue to surround and hold us in Your loving and sustaining care. Help us to learn from Your compassion and faithful presence as we reach out to share these same things with others in our lives. Amen

July 14

REFLECTION

Come to me, all you who labor and are burdened, and I will give you rest. *(Matthew 11:28)* When and how will I plan to take a few moments to rest a bit in my day and open myself to hear and feel what is good and gentle around me?

PRAYER

God, Gentle Shepherd, thank You for reminding us to take a few moments in our day to be still, to take a few deep breaths, and to rest. In these moments, ease our burdens, clear our minds and hearts so that we can gain a new perspective in our work and relationships. Amen

July 15

REFLECTION

Mercy, both given and received, is one of the greatest gifts of healing for the human spirit. How have I experienced mercy in my life? What has been its healing power for me?

PRAYER

God of Mercy, guide us to not play "god", but to let You be God in our lives and in the lives of those we relate with each day. Help us to learn from Your mercy and forgiveness in our lives, and from those who have shown mercy to us along the way as well. Amen

July 16

REFLECTION

Life is strengthened and sustained by many healthy friendships. To love and to be loved is one of the greatest gifts of human existence. What do I consider the healthy and supportive friendships in my life? How did these come to be?

PRAYER

Faithful God, thank You for the friendships in our lives which strengthen and sustain the goodness You have placed within us. May the love we share be genuine and self-less in our giving and human care. Amen

July 17

REFLECTION

When we sow seeds of kindness and encouragement to another person, we may be blessing them with the hope and strength they need to deal with the weeds and struggles of life. Do my words and behaviors toward others bring kindness or hurt?

PRAYER

Ever-Present God, touch my heart so that my interactions with others always bring kindness, hope, and encouragement. Amen

July 18

REFLECTION

My strength and my courage is the Lord; God has been my refuge and my savior *(Exodus 15)* What times in my life have I experienced God being my strength, my courage, my refuge, and my savior?

PRAYER

Gracious God, in every age and time You desire to bring us strength, courage, and hope. Guide us today that we might also bring strength, courage, and hope to all in our care. Amen

July 19

REFLECTION

We most often experience and come to know the compassion and kindness of God through other persons in our lives. Who in my life has reflected to me and others the compassion and kindness of God? Do others also experience this from me?

PRAYER

Merciful and Gracious God, guide us to reflect on our own behavior and interactions with others. Help us to be aware of our own anger or times of feeling insecure so that we do not inflict unnecessary pain or harsh words on others. Soften our spirits with kindness and compassion. Amen

July 20

REFLECTION

We may fall and make mistakes many times in our lives, but we may not really be a failure until we begin to blame someone else. How do I deal with the mistakes and errors in my life?

PRAYER

Forgiving God, thank You for the times You guide me to see my mistakes, to humbly own them and start anew. Help me to learn from the many experiences of my life so that I might grow in wisdom, integrity, and compassion for others. Amen

July 21

REFLECTION

What is the right and honest thing to do can sometimes be dismissed for what is more convenient. Where do my choices and behaviors lean… toward what is the right and honest thing to do or toward what is more convenient at the time?

PRAYER

God of Truth, guide each of us to live with inner integrity in all we say and do. Give us strength to do what is right and honest in our work and in all our relationships even when it is not always convenient at the time. Amen

July 22

REFLECTION

True care inspires and gently reassures us. Giving us a feeling of support, it reinforces our connection with others. It can be one of the best things we can do for our health, whether we're giving or receiving it. How do I offer true care and support to others? How and from whom do I receive it?

PRAYER

Supporting and Sustaining God, thank You for the ways You lead us to truly give care and support to others around us. Thank You for those in my life whose care encourages and reassures me, helping me to be wholesome and healthy. Amen

July 23

REFLECTION

To a happy person, the formula for happiness may simply be: Regardless of what happened early this morning, last week, or last year - or what may happen later this evening, tomorrow, or in two years - now in the present is where happiness is found and enjoyed. In what times and places do I seek to find happiness in my life?

PRAYER

God of Joy, teach us how to live more in the present moment and receive each new day as a precious gift to be treasured and lived well. May happiness be felt in our hearts and shared in ways which lift the hearts of others. Amen

July 24

REFLECTION

In the Scriptures *(1 Kings3; 5, 7-12)* God invites Solomon, "Ask something of me and I will give it to you." As one chosen to serve God's people, Solomon's request was, "Give your servant an understanding heart to lead your people and to distinguish right from wrong." Perhaps this is one of the "pearls of great price" which Jesus encourages all of us to search for in our lives? What do I ask of God today?

PRAYER

God of the Sabbath, give each of us understanding and wisdom as we seek to serve your people, our families, and our co-workers. Help us always to know right from wrong and to walk always in ways which please You. Amen

July 25

REFLECTION

There is no need for them to go away; give them some food your-selves. *(Matthew 14:16)* How might God be calling me to care for and give "food' to someone today… the food of kindness, understanding, listening, or food for their physical or spiritual needs?

PRAYER

Ever-Present God, You sustain and provide for us in so many ways each day. Slow us down and give us the awareness and generosity of spirit to do the same for those we encounter today. Amen

July 26

REFLECTION

Is it through Moses alone that the Lord speaks? Does God not speak through us also? *(Numbers 12:2)* Who may God use to speak to me today? Will I be open enough to listen? How might God also use me as an instrument to speak God's word or message to another?

PRAYER

God of all time, You have spoken and guided Your people in every time and every age. Open our eyes and hearts to recognize the ways and the times You desire to speak Your word of hope, comfort, inspiration, or challenge to us and through us. Give us the strength and courage to say and do always what is right and true in Your sight. Amen

July 27

REFLECTION

Sometimes we can be robbed by two thieves – regrets of the past or fear of the future. How does either of these sometimes rob me of how I am able to live more fully and peacefully in the present?

PRAYER

God-with-us, free us from the ways we may be robbed or held bound by regrets of the past or fear of the future. Open us to trust more fully in You and the blessings You share with us each day. Amen

July 28

REFLECTION

The integration of prayer with daily living is something which the wise ones of most faith traditions promote and encourage for harmony and balance in one's life. When this becomes an integral in our lives, we often find we can handle in a more peaceful way the many situations which we are called to face each day. How do I make prayer a part of my life?

PRAYER

Ever-Present God, teach me to pray and to grow in my relationship with You. May quiet moments of prayer and reflection come to me as easily as gently breathing in and breathing out, refreshing my spirit, my mind, and my heart. Thank You for patiently waiting for each of us to open ourselves to You and the life You desire to share. Amen

July 29

REFLECTION

O God, your way is holy. You are the God who works wonders; among the peoples you have shown your power. *(Psalm 11:14-15)* What wonders have I seen God working in my life or in the lives of those I love or care for?

PRAYER

Wondrous God, we praise and thank You for Your presence and action in our lives. You provide and care for us in many small as well as big ways as we walk our journey of life. Open our eyes to see Your wonders today and live with thankful hearts. Amen

July 30

REFLECTION

None of us can go back and change the past, but any of us can start today and make a new beginning. What will I do with the gift of life and the opportunities I am given today?

PRAYER

God, Ever-New, thank You for the gift of life and the potential for new beginnings we are given with each new day. Inspire us to know how to move on from the past and welcome the new opportunities for life and service You offer us every day. Amen

July 31

REFLECTION

In a Gospel event *(Matthew 14:22-36)* when the disciples were being tossed about by the waves while they were in a boat on the lake, Jesus came toward them and said, "Take courage, it is I; do not be afraid." Have there been times in my life recently when I have felt tossed and turned by the waves of life, stresses or struggles? What has helped me to have courage and not be afraid?

PRAYER

Sustaining God, thank You for your faithful presence and those whom You have placed in my life who help me to find courage and not be afraid when I feel tossed and turned by the waves, stress, and difficulties of life. Bless and sustain each of us on our journeys through life. Amen

August

August 1

REFLECTION

Whoever sows sparingly will also reap sparingly; whoever sows bountifully, will also reap bountifully. God loves a cheerful giver. God is able to make every grace abundant for you, so that in all things, always having all you need, you may have an abundance for every good work. *(2 Corinthians 9:6-8)* How would my spirit of giving be rated by my family and co-workers, sparing or abundant...cheerful or half-hearted?

PRAYER

Generous God, You give us not all that we want, but truly all we need as we live and work each day. Give us generous and trusting spirits so that we can receive from Your abundance and give to others with cheerful and caring hearts this day. Amen

August 2

REFLECTION

In the Hebrew Scriptures *(1Kings 19:4-8),* when Elijah was weary from the journey and felt he could not go on, God sent an angel to bring him just enough food and drink to sustain and strengthen him. Have there been times in my life when I felt weary, tired, or discouraged? In what ways did God send an "angel" or provide something to sustain, strengthen, or lift me up in those times?

PRAYER

Ever-Present God, thank You for all the ways You enter our lives to sustain, strengthen, and provide for us on our journeys. When we feel tired, discouraged, or weary, open our eyes to see how You are there giving us just what we need in those times. Amen

August 3

REFLECTION

Where two or three are gathered in my name, there I am in the midst of them. *(Matthew 18:20)* As we live and work together in our faith-based ministry, we gather and serve in God's name. How do I experience and contribute to this environment of spirituality (God-with-us) as we serve together each day?

PRAYER

Loving God, You live within us and among us as we gather in Your name to serve each day. May all we do reflect Your presence and Your healing care for those we serve and work among. Amen.

August 4

REFLECTION

Some things have to be believed in order to be seen. What good will I see today because I believe in the possibilities of it happening? What might I miss or not see today because I don't believe it could be?

PRAYER

God of infinite possibilities, touch our hearts and increase our faith to believe in, see, and experience all the good You place in our lives and our relationships each day. Help us to see more because we have come to believe. Amen

August 5

REFLECTION

You can't shake hands with a clenched fist. If or when you find yourself feeling up tight with your hands or your heart clenched, what do you do to help yourself grow into a posture of welcome and openness?

PRAYER

Freeing God, make us aware of our own attitudes, manner, and body language as we interact with others in our day. Transform us to welcome and serve others with a spirit of openness and peace. Amen

August 6

REFLECTION

Jesus took Peter, James, and John up a high mountain apart by themselves. He was transfigured before them and his clothes became dazzling white. Peter said in amazement, "Rabbi, it is good for us to be here!" *(Mark 9:2,5)* What are the times and places in my life when I have felt or said, "God, it is good for me to be here?"

PRAYER

Revealing God, thank You for the times of insight, vision, understanding and transformation You have brought into our lives. Thank You for the times we have been refreshed and renewed, feeling "It is truly good for us to be here!" Amen

August 7

REFLECTION

The "Sabbath" day is something which is at the heart of one's spiritual life. Time given for rest and communing with God is never time lost, but actually time gained so that our relationships and our whole life may become more deeply human and sprinkled with the Divine. When and how do I spend "Sabbath" time in my life?

PRAYER

Creator God, You have blessed us with all You have made on the earth and in the heavens. You have also blessed us with the gift of "Sabbath" time which You created and enjoy Yourself. Guide us to embrace, plan for, and use "Sabbath" days and times in our lives to rest and be renewed in our relationship with You, our family, friends, co-workers, and all we serve. Amen

August 8

REFLECTION

People, even more than things, have to be restored, renewed, revived, reclaimed, and redeemed; never throw out or completely give up on anyone. Who has been God's instrument in restoring, reviving, or renewing me when I needed it? Who might need this kind of care and compassion from me today?

PRAYER

Redeeming God, thank You for the persons You have placed in our lives as instruments of healing, understanding, and compassion. Soften our hearts so that You can use us as Your instruments in these ways for others as well. Amen

August 9

REFLECTION

All truths are easy to understand once they are discovered; the point is to discover them. *(Galileo Galilei)* Am I open and ready to learn and ponder the deeper truths of life? Or do I tend to live more on the surface of life and hold to those things which are mostly more convenient for me?

PRAYER

God of Truth, show us how to seek and discover the deeper truths of life, beauty, and goodness in our relationships with You, with those persons we interact with each day, and within ourselves. Help us to see as You see and to understand as You understand. Amen

August 10

REFLECTION

The most beautiful things in the world cannot be seen or even touched. They must be felt with the heart. *(Helen Keller)* Do I mostly live and act from my "head" or from my "heart"? How can I practice a healthy balance of both?

PRAYER

God of Beauty, teach us how to live in wonder and awareness of those things which can only be known and felt with our hearts. Give us a sense of reverence for the truly beautiful things in life which have the power to touch our inner self when we slow down to experience and receive them. Amen

August 11

REFLECTION

May Almighty God bless you. May God look upon you with the eyes of great mercy and given you much peace. May God pour forth all graces on you abundantly, and in heaven may God place you among the saints. (*St. Clare of Assisi*) As I go through my day, do I look upon others with kindness and wish them God's blessings and peace?

PRAYER

Gracious God, You shower us each day with an abundance of blessings. Thank you for Your care and direction in our lives. Help us to look upon each person we encounter today with kindness, asking Your blessings for them as well. Amen

August 12

REFLECTION

Everything can be taken from a person but one thing; the last of the human freedoms - to choose one's attitude in any given set of circumstances. (*Victor Frankl*) What attitude do I choose, nurture, and try to sustain within myself each day?

PRAYER

God of Life, guide us each day to choose and live with an attitude of gratitude. Fill us with a positive attitude toward life and other persons as we seek to give of ourselves in serving You and those who come to us in need of healing. Amen

August 13

REFLECTION

Everybody needs beauty as well as bread, places to play in and pray in, where nature may heal and cheer and give strength to the body and soul alike. Where do I find beauty, places to play and pray, places where nature heals and relaxes me, giving strength to my body and soul alike? Do I give myself time for these things in my life?

PRAYER

God of Sabbath Times, You have created places of beauty in our world where we can go to rest, find peace, and renew our bodies, minds, and souls. Guide us to seek balance and harmony in our lives so that we may be refreshed in honoring the precious gift of life which You have given to each of us. Amen

August 14

REFLECTION

You never know when one act of kindness or one word of encouragement might change a life forever. How will my interactions with others today influence or change their lives in a positive or negative way?

PRAYER

Life-Giving God, guide our actions and our words each day so that we may lift up the hearts of those we meet in ways which bring them hope, encouragement, and healing. Amen

August 15

REFLECTION

This Feast Day celebrates Mary being taken up body and soul into heaven when her earthly life was completed. It is celebrated each year at this time when the fullness of the harvest from our gardens and fields is being enjoyed. We live with the same hope and promise that God will also gather each of us into the harvest and fullness of heaven at the time of our death. What is my hope and belief about life after death?

PRAYER

Eternal and Life-giving God, thank You for the harvest of fresh produce we have been enjoying from earth's gardens, fields, and orchards this year. Guide each of us to live as faithful and true disciples during our time on earth, so that we may enjoy the full harvest of eternal life with You when our journey here is completed. Amen

August 16

REFLECTION

A spirituality of gentleness flows from a great inner strength, and a strong respect and reverence for others. It is fostered by an attitude of non-judgment and a conviction that each person we meet is to be treated with dignity and acceptance. Do I have an inner strength of character which shows itself in a spirit of gentleness with others?

PRAYER

God of Gentleness, create in us the inner strength of character and self which overflows with respect, reverence, and gentleness toward all we interact with each day. Guide us to empower and not power-over as we serve in Your name. Amen

August 17

REFLECTION

Appreciating each other is a true human value, one that can ease much of the stress in our relationships and help strengthen the universal bond among all those we interact with or influence. How freely do I show appreciation and gratitude to my co-workers, family members, and friends?

PRAYER

Gracious God, guide our hearts and our actions each day so that we may find ways of showing appreciation and encouragement to those around us. Help us to bring hope and kindness to ease the stress and pressures of life. Amen

August 18

REFLECTION

Sometimes when we are with people on a daily or regular basis, we tend to think we know them well. We may subconsciously label them and have a positive or negative way of viewing them. What could happen if we let go of our labels and biased ways of seeing others? How can we open ourselves to see others in new and freeing ways?

PRAYER

God our Creator, open our eyes and free us of our biases so that we may see the beauty and goodness of those we live and work with, and those we are called to serve each day. Help us to see as You see, understand as You understand, and love as You love. Amen

August 19

REFLECTION

One loving heart sets another on fire. Attitudes can be contagious… is mine worth catching?

PRAYER

Loving God, set our hearts on fire with the love, compassion, and mercy You give to each of us every day. May all we do reflect Your goodness and presence within us and among us as we serve Your people in need. Amen

August 20

REFLECTION

The human brain and heart are wired to be loving. Sometimes we do not activate or nurture this innate gift. Life experiences can wound people so deeply that the power to love is wounded too. How do I activate and enliven my own innate gift to be a loving person? What do I do to heal any hurts I carry which may have wounded my power to love?

Creator God, You have created each of us in Your own image and likeness to be loving in all our relationships. Heal any wounds we may have which can diminish our power to be loving and kind to the people in our lives each day. Amen

August 21

REFLECTION

It is not how much you do, but how much love you put into what you do that matters. *(Mother Teresa of Calcutta)* As I go through the activities of my day, do I find myself mainly just going through the motions or do I give of myself with great interest, care, and love?

PRAYER

Life-Giving God, infuse in us the positive energy, love, and compassion we need to give of ourselves in full and unselfish ways as we serve and work with others. Amen

August 22

REFLECTION

The pessimist complains about the wind; the optimist expects it to change; the realist adjusts the sails. As unexpected interruptions or situations come into my life and my day, how do I usually respond and deal with them?

PRAYER

Ever- Present God, it seems that the norm of our day can often be experiencing interruptions and situations we had not expected. Give us the wisdom and inner peace to know how to respond and deal with all that comes our way. Amen

August 23

REFLECTION

All of you are children of light. Therefore encourage one another and build one another up. *(1 Thessalonians 5:5, 11)* Do others see me as a person of light and hope, encouraging and building up those I interact with each day?

PRAYER

God of Light, we ask that the glow of Your presence may be seen in each of us as we serve those in need and as we collaborate with our co-workers. Let our words and our actions bring encouragement and hope to all. Amen

August 24

REFLECTION

There is only one thing necessary: to be what God wants us to be. *(Thomas Merton)* As I reflect on my life, the work and relationships I am involved in, does it seem to be what God has called me to do and be?

PRAYER

Creator God, guide each of us to know and to be what you have created us to be. May we use the precious gift of life given to us in ways which bring life, hope, and healing care to all we live with, serve, and work among. Amen

August 25

REFLECTION

The best way to find yourself is to lose yourself in the service of others. *(Mahatma Gandhi)* When and how do I find and know my true self? Is my life all about me or is it truly about giving and serving others? How do I assess this?

PRAYER

God-with-us, thank You for the life, abilities, and talents You have given to each of us. Guide us to use these and to give ourselves in the service of others around us. May our giving be a reflection of Your life within us. Amen

August 26

REFLECTION

A loving person lives in a loving world. A hostile person lives in a hostile world. Our attitudes and manner of relating are often reflected back to us and will color our day. What kind of attitude and way of relating do I bring to my interactions with others?

PRAYER

Loving God, direct our hearts, our attitudes, and our manner of relating so that all we do helps to create a loving and positive world for ourselves and all around us. Amen

August 27

REFLECTION

Our hearts are restless until they rest in God. (*St. Augustine*) In what ways do I feel restless, dissatisfied, empty, or in search of something more in my life?

PRAYER

Creator God, give our hearts peace as we strive to center our lives in a faithful relationship with You. Bring us back when we seek after all that only brings us emptiness or a restless heart. Amen

August 28

REFLECTION

Worry never robs tomorrow of its sorrow, it only drains today of its joy. What are the things I tend to worry or get upset about? Do I have the ability or power to change them? If not, why do I allow them to overshadow the joy I could have today?

PRAYER

Faithful God, give us the serenity to accept the things we cannot change, the courage to change the things we can, and the wisdom to know the difference. Open us to find joy in the simple blessings within each day, and always give thanks to You. Amen

August 29

REFLECTION

In the Christian Scriptures, the Letter of James 2:1 tells us that we may judge falsely when we assess the quality or worth of a person by the clothes they wear or by their external appearance. What we initially see can divert us from seeing both the internal goodness and the external disguise of a person or situation. How do I tend to judge or assess persons I meet?

PRAYER

Creator God, open our eyes and our hearts so that we may look beyond the outward appearances of those we serve and work with. Open us to see the real person within and relate to them with reverence and respect. Amen

August 30

REFLECTION

Courage is not always the opposite of fear, but rather the judgment that there is something else more important and worthwhile to do than be controlled by fear. When have I been called to act with courage in recent weeks?

Life-Giving God, bless each of us with the courage and strength we need to act beyond our fears when events in our lives call us to do what is right and good for those in need and for ourselves as well. Amen

August 31

REFLECTION

What we do is less than a drop in the ocean. But if that drop was missing, the ocean would lack something important. *(Mother Teresa of Calcutta)* Do I see God using me as an instrument bringing something important and good to my part of this world?

PRAYER

Great and Awesome God, You have created each of us for a purpose and a reason. Guide us to know the meaning and purpose of our lives so that we may make our contribution in this world and serve always with generous and grateful hearts. Amen

September

September 1

REFLECTION

If we seek God in all things, we will find God always by our side. Is one of my desires to seek and find God in all things and in all the events of my day?

PRAYER

Ever-Present God, instill in us the desire and the ability to seek and find You in all the events and situations of our lives. Let us experience Your presence and guidance with and among us as we make important decisions, and as we seek to serve others with compassion and excellence. Amen

September 2

REFLECTION

Why do you notice the splinter in your brother's eye, but do not perceive the wooden beam in your own? *(Luke 6:41)* Our own blindness or limitations can cause us to lose our focus in seeing the beauty and goodness in others around us. How clear has my vision been lately?

God of Light, guide us to live and see with Your light, so that we are not caught in our own blindness. Help us to be merciful and compassionate with others as You are with each of us. Amen

September 3

REFLECTION

Every tree is known by the good fruit that it bears. The tree that is beside the running water is fresher and gives more fruit. *(St. Teresa of Avila)* What life-giving waters help to refresh me so that I may bear good fruit in my life and work?

PRAYER

Life-Giving God, help us to be reflective in caring for ourselves so that we may be healthy and wise in ways which make it possible for us to bear good fruit in our lives for You and for the good of those we serve. Amen

September 4

REFLECTION

How would I describe my relationship with God at this time in my life? On an "as needed" basis; pretty solid and nurtured daily; or not much there on my end right now? How has it come to be this way?

PRAYER

Faithful God, be with me as I reflect on my relationship with You at this time in my life. Give me insight and wisdom to see how You walk the path of life with me each day and invite me into a deeper relationship with You. Amen

September 5

REFLECTION

For where two or three are gathered together in my name, there am I in the midst of them. *(Matthew 18:20)* We come together each day in God's name and as God's people to pray and to serve the needs of those who come to us in our ministry. How will I experience God present and acting in our midst today?

PRAYER

Ever-Present God, make us aware of Your presence and direction in our lives as we come to serve the sick, the injured, the poor and vulnerable who enter our lives today. Give us hearts of compassion and tender care. Amen

September 6

REFLECTION

May the goodness of the Lord be upon us, and give success to the work of our hands. *(Psalm 89:17)* How often do I stop to thank God for the work, job, health and skills I have which help to provide for my own needs and those of my family?

PRAYER

Life-Giving God, thank You for the talents and abilities You have given to each of us as we serve together in Your name. Continue to bless the work of our hands, our minds, and our hearts as we seek to do our best for all those who come to us in need. Amen

September 7

REFLECTION

As we look back in our lives, perhaps the times we feel we have really lived fully are the times when we have acted in a spirit of love and care for others. How do I want to feel as I look back at the end of this day?

Eternal God, place within me today a spirit of mercy, compassion, and understanding toward all I will interact with and serve. At the end of my day, I desire to feel that I have lived and served well. Amen

September 8

REFLECTION

God uses ordinary people to help change the world… not super humans or geniuses, but usually ordinary people. How will I invite God to work in me to change someone's world, to make a difference in someone's life today?

PRAYER

Faithful God, use us as Your instruments today in ways that will bring hope, kindness, and healing to others. Help us to change someone's world, someone's life in a positive and uplifting way each day. Amen

September 9

REFLECTION

Do not judge and you will not be judged. Do not condemn, and you will not be condemned. Forgive and you will be forgiven. Give and gifts will be given to you. For the measure with which you measure will in turn be measured out to you. *(Luke 6:37-38)* What will be my attitude toward others today?

PRAYER

God of Mercy, guide my thoughts and my attitude today as I interact with my co-workers and those we serve. Help me to be generous in offering mercy, patience and understanding to those I'm with today. Amen

September 10

REFLECTION

In the presence of hope, faith is born. In the presence of faith, love becomes a possibility. In the presence of love, miracles can happen. How are hope, faith, and love expressed in my life each day?

PRAYER

Loving God, refresh my life with hope, faith, and love today so that the good You desire can happen through my service and care for others in need. Amen

September 11

REFLECTION

If there is any one secret of success, it lies in the ability to get the other person's point of view and see things from that person's angle as well as from your own. *(Henry Ford)* How successful am I with truly listening, in trying to see and understand another person's point of view and experience?

PRAYER

God of Mercy and Understanding, open our eyes and soften our hearts as we work and interact with other people each day. Give us the power of true listening and openness in inviting and receiving the view and experience of others, as we serve together and seek to make wise and compassionate decisions. Amen

September 12

REFLECTION

Whoever wishes to be first must be last of all and the servant of all. *(Mark 9:35)* In what ways or times do I sometimes tend to put myself first or take care of myself first when I need to step back and become the one who serves?

God of Humble Service, You washed the feet of Your disciples and call each of us to live in this same posture of service and care toward one another. When we begin to get full of ourselves and focused on our own needs, nudge us and call us back to generous service in Your name. Amen

September 13

REFLECTION

As Jesus passed by, he saw a man named Matthew sitting at the customs post. He said to him, "Follow me." Matthew got up to follow him. *(Matthew 9:9)* In what ways or times have I experienced God calling my name to walk more closely with God in my life?

PRAYER

Inviting God, quiet my heart and my mind so that I can hear You call my name in the events of my life. Help me to know the ways You desire for me to go and how to walk in truth and goodness with You each day. Amen

September 14

REFLECTION

Humility is the mother of many virtues, because from it charity, reverence, patience, and peace are born. One who is humble is eager to listen, seeks to offend no one, desires to be at peace with everyone, and is kind toward all.

PRAYER

God-with-us, guide us to live with humility, reverence, and patience in all our interactions with others. Give us hearts of compassion and kindness toward all persons. Amen

September 15

REFLECTION

I was 14 when my father died. I miss everything about him. He taught us that we shouldn't be people of success; we should be people of values, because that is the only thing that endures. *(Robert F. Kennedy, Jr.)* What is my goal in life…to seek success or to be a person rooted in values?

PRAYER

Creator God, give success to the work of our hands and our work. Yet let it be because we have chosen to be rooted in the deeper values You desire for us to embrace and live as we serve in Your name. Amen

September 16

REFLECTION

Sometimes life can be so busy, yet the business may involve so much motion and activity that at the end of the day we may find that we just feel unsatisfied, empty, and exhausted, wondering what our day was really all about. How can I focus my day and my heart to help me find meaning and purpose in what I do?

PRAYER

Life-Giving God, touch our hearts, our minds, and our spirits so that we may reflect upon and find meaning, purpose, encouragement, and a sense of positive satisfaction in what we do each day. Guide us to serve others with the joy and energy which come from this reflection and awareness. Amen

September 17

REFLECTION

No matter how much we exert ourselves, people will never have faith in us unless we show them charity and compassion. *(St. Vincent de Paul)* In all the work and effort I put forth each day, do others experience love and compassion in me?

PRAYER

God of Love, in the business of our days, guide us to live and work always in a spirit of true charity and compassion. May all we do reflect Your presence and love to those we serve. Amen

September 18

REFLECTION

Never doubt that a small group of thoughtful, committed people can change the world. Indeed it's the only thing that ever has. *(Margaret Meade)* In what ways do I work with others to make a positive difference that may ripple out to help change our world?

PRAYER

God, Ever-Present, guide our hearts and minds so that we may work with others to help create a better place and life-giving situations for those we serve and work among. Amen

September 19

REFLECTION

The person who is trustworthy in small matters is also trustworthy in great ones. *(Luke 16:10)* Does my behavior show that I am trustworthy in small and in greater matters in my life?

PRAYER

All-Knowing God, direct my heart and my behaviors. May I be truly trustworthy in all my responsibilities and relationships each day. Amen

September 20

REFLECTION

Come now, let us engage ourselves with renewed love to serve the poor, and let us even seek out the poorest and most abandoned of all. *(St. Vincent de Paul)* Who will be the poor I may be called to serve today… those without insurance, those who have received a difficult health diagnosis, those who have lost a loved one, those who feel afraid or alone?

PRAYER

Fill us, God, with fresh enthusiasm and compassion in our service of Your poor ones. Keep us faithful in living the Gospel values each day. Help us to share Your love and compassion with all we serve and work among. Amen

September 21

REFLECTION

It is from your hands that Our Lord, in the person of the sick, seeks relief. *(St. Vincent de Paul)* How will my hands, my touch, and the care I give serve others with tenderness, understanding, and compassion today?

PRAYER

Gracious God, help us to make time today to serve You in those who are most in need of encouragement, love, and assistance. Amen

September 22

REFLECTION

Be watchful that nothing in your use be damaged or spoiled. *(St. Vincent de Paul)* All the materials, resources, tools and technology we have are placed in our care with trust. How well do we use all of these to serve the needs of others each day?

Generous God, guide us each day to be good stewards of our time, our talents, and the resources we have as we serve all persons entrusted to our care. Amen

September 23

REFLECTION
Put yourself in the patient's place and imagine how you would feel. *(St. Vincent de Paul)* In all we do, let us treat others as we would want to be treated and as we would want our family and loved ones to be treated.

PRAYER
God, keep us aware of all those special needs, often not expressed but so much appreciated when attended to, in those who suffer. Amen

September 24

REFLECTION
You represent the goodness of God to the sick. *(St. Vincent de Paul)* How will the sick and the vulnerable experience the goodness of God in my interactions with them today?

PRAYER
God of Compassion, we ask that all we do will represent and reflect Your goodness and care for others each day. Amen

September 25

REFLECTION
God has created each of us for a definite purpose and service in our lives. We are each a link in a chain, a bond of connection between persons, to attend to and provide for the common good of all. What purpose and service do I recognize I have been created to contribute and provide for the common good of those around me?

PRAYER

Here I am, God. Guide and direct me today that I may more clearly see the purpose and meaning of my life, and the service You are calling me to offer for the good of those I serve, work with, and live among. Amen

September 26

REFLECTION

It's not the things you get, but the hearts you touch that will determine your success. In what ways do I touch the hearts and lives of others bringing kindness, encouragement, hope, and life to them?

PRAYER

Loving God, help us to know the ways that You call us to make a positive difference in the lives of those we interact with each day… our family, friends, co-workers, and all those we serve and care for in Your name. Amen

September 27

REFLECTION

View the actions of your neighbor in a spirit of charity; should their actions have a hundred sides, always look at the best in them. *(St. Vincent de Paul)* In what spirit do I view the actions of my co-workers, the individuals and families we serve? Do I look upon them with charity or in more negative ways?

PRAYER

God of Compassion, give us a spirit of charity and eyes of understanding so that we can treat others with kindness and generosity each day. Knowing that we have not walked in another person's shoes, keep us from judging others in harsh or impatient ways. Amen

September 28

REFLECTION

The longer we live the more we may discover that a waste of life lies in the love we have not given, the talents we have not developed or shared, the prejudices we hold on to. What can I do to open my life and my heart to live and give myself more fully?

PRAYER

Life-Giving God, guide us to live our lives as fully as we can through the love we freely give, in using our talents and skill to serve others, and in freeing ourselves of any prejudices which hold us bound. Amen

September 29

REFLECTION

Try to stay positive. We become what we think about and dwell on in our minds. What do I fill my minds and thoughts with as I go through my day?

PRAYER

Transforming God, direct our minds and our hearts that we may be filled with what is hopeful, positive, and good. Transform us anew each day into Your own image and likeness as we serve and work together. Amen

September 30

REFLECTION

Courage does not always roar. Sometimes it is the quiet voice at the end of the day saying, "I will try again tomorrow." When and how do I experience courage in my life?

PRAYER

God of Courage, give us the strength and wisdom we need each day to try again and stay the course when situations and events become more challenging. Help us to engage in good self-care so that we can stay healthy and reverence the precious gift of life which You have given to each of us. Amen

October

October 1

REFLECTION

Do all things with love and a willing heart today. Some of what you do may seem small or insignificant to you, but it may be big and very significant in the life of another. What is my attitude and manner as I serve and interact with others each day?

PRAYER

Creator God, help me to do all things well today no matter how small or insignificant some of these may seem. Help me to recognize that what is routine or daily to me may help to change or bring joy or comfort to someone else's life this day. Amen

October 2

REFLECTION

I believe there are angels among us sent to us from somewhere up above. They come to us in our darkest hours to show us how to live, to teach us how to give, to guide us with their light and words of love. Who are the "angels" God will send into your life today? Will God use you as an "angel" for someone in need today?

PRAYER

Loving God, thank You for those You send into our lives who bring light, guidance, and comfort just at the right time. Use us as Your instruments and messengers for those in need this day. Amen

October 3

REFLECTION

In the Christian Scriptures *(Luke 10:25-37),* we read the story of a traveler who has been called the "Good Samaritan" because he stopped to help someone along the way who was injured and in need. How might I be called to be a Good Samaritan for someone I encounter today? Can I think of a time when someone was truly a Good Samaritan to me?

PRAYER

God of Compassion, open our eyes and our hearts to become aware of those along our way today who may need us to stop and assist them or go the extra mile to meet their needs. Give us generous and caring attitudes in all we do. Amen

October 4

REFLECTION

Preach the Gospel always. When necessary, use words. *(St. Francis of Assisi)* Do my daily actions and behaviors always match the words I speak and the values I claim to be living?

PRAYER

Lord, make me an instrument of Your peace. Where there is hatred, help me bring love. Where there is sadness, let me bring joy. Where there is darkness, help me bring light. Where there is hurt, let me bring healing. Amen

October 5

REFLECTION

Be alert and discerning in your life so that the things that matter most are not neglected for the things that matter the least. How do I help myself hold to and give time for the important priorities in my life?

PRAYER

Eternal God, guide us to take the time we need to be quiet and reflective so that we can assess our priorities. May we find life-giving energy in doing what we know are the more important things which help us nurture and sustain healthy and good relationships. Amen

October 6

REFLECTION

We do not receive wisdom; we discover it within ourselves as we journey through struggles, uncertainty, and times of darkness. What pearls of wisdom have I discovered along my own journey and how have these helped to re-focus my choices and decisions?

PRAYER

God of Wisdom, guide us to learn from our own struggles, mistakes, and times of darkness. May new insights and understanding come to us as we take time to be quiet and reflective, finding You always near to direct us. Amen

October 7

REFLECTION

Give us each day our daily bread. *(Luke 11:3)* What is the "bread" that nourishes and sustains me each day at work and in my personal life? Kindness, encouragement, inner peace, prayer, moments of quiet, relationships with others....?

PRAYER

Give us today, Gracious God, the daily bread we need to live and serve well. You are the source of all good things. Nourish each of us and sustain us as we journey through this day. Amen

October 8

REFLECTION

Let yourself be silently drawn by the stronger pull of what you really love and know is right to do. How and where are my heart and my spirit being drawn today?

PRAYER

Ever-Present God, make us aware of the silent yet sure ways You call us each day. Give us the grace to respond in ways which move us toward what we know is right and good for ourselves and for those we love and serve each day. Amen

October 9

REFLECTION

Blessed are those who hear the word of God, take it to heart and live it. *(Luke 11:28)* In what ways do I open myself to hear the word of God in my life? In what ways do I embrace and live what God's message calls me to?

PRAYER

Life-Giving God, open our ears and our hearts to hear Your message and Your guidance in our lives. Open us especially to receive Your word when it may come in unexpected ways and through unexpected events or persons. Amen

October 10

REFLECTION

I prayed, and prudence was given me; I pleaded, and the spirit of wisdom came to me. *(Wisdom 7:7)* In the midst of life's journey and times of important decision-making, do I pause to ask God for the gifts of prudence and wisdom to guide me?

PRAYER

God of Light and Insight, direct our minds and our decisions each day with Your gifts of prudence and wisdom. May all we do reveal that we are living and serving in Your ways. Amen

October 11

REFLECTION

Sometimes in the midst of our struggles, doubts, confusion, pain, God may invite us to "sing a new song" or walk in a new direction. Might God be calling me to "sing a new song" or walk a new direction in my life at this time?

PRAYER

Renewing God, refresh our spirits and re-direct our thoughts and steps in times of struggle, doubt, confusion, or pain. Nudge us to know the times You are calling us to "sing a new song" so that all we do reflects Your presence and compassion in our lives. Amen

October 12

REFLECTION

Did not the maker of the outside also make the inside? *(Luke 11:40)* When I look at and relate with another person, do I most often focus on what I see externally… physical appearance, clothes, title or position; or do I stop to look deeper and desire to see the inner goodness and beauty of each person?

Creator God, guide us to see as You see, understand as You understand, and love as You love, as we work with each other and serve those who come to us in need of healing and compassion. Amen

October 13

REFLECTION

How wonderful it is that nobody need wait a single moment before starting to improve the world. *(Anne Frank)* In what small or even bigger ways might I be called to start making an improvement in my corner of the world today?

PRAYER

Ever-Present God, open our eyes and our hearts to realize the potential we have every moment to make a positive difference in the lives of those we serve and work among. Help us to remember that goodness and love begin with us. Amen

October 14

REFLECTION

May Your kindness, O Lord, be upon us as we place our trust in You. *(Psalm 33:22)* In what ways am I being called to put my trust in God and God's direction in my life today?

PRAYER

Gracious God, touch our hearts and remind us to place our trust in You as we work together in Your name. Open our eyes so that we can see Your kindness in our lives and in the lives of those we serve this day. Amen

October 15

REFLECTION

No one is so advanced in prayer that they do not often have to return to the beginning. *(St. Teresa of Avila)* How might God be calling me to renew my spirit of prayer and my relationship with God and my neighbor at this time in my life?

PRAYER

Gracious God, teach us anew how to pray and how to be in right relationship with You and all those You have placed in our lives. Amen

October 16

REFLECTION

We are each called to be a vessel where God can dwell. In what ways do I open and prepare myself so that God can live and move and transform my life for good?

PRAYER

Indwelling God, awaken us to Your presence within us and within all those around us today. Transform us anew each day into Your image and likeness as we strive to bring healing and understanding to those we serve. Amen

October 17

REFLECTION

Preconceived notions and assumptions can become locks on the door to wisdom and true understanding. How often do preconceived notions and assumptions blind me from truly seeing and understanding other persons?

PRAYER

God of Truth, free us from any preconceived notions or assumptions about person or situations which may blind us from truly seeing, understanding, and acting with wisdom and right judgment in our lives. Amen

October 18

REFLECTION

It's important to trust and believe in people, or life can come to feel impossible and empty. What is generally my attitude toward those I work with and interact with each day? Do I open myself to trust and believe in their goodness?

PRAYER

Creator God, thank You for trusting and believing in us, created in Your own image and likeness. Open our eyes and our hearts to grow in trust and openness, as we serve and work together in Your name. Amen

October 19

REFLECTION

The very possibility of friendship with God can transfigure our life and the potential for every human friendship. How would I assess my relationship with God at this time? How does it enrich my life and my faith journey?

PRAYER

God, Faithful Friend and Companion, thank You for being with us each day as we journey through life. Touch our hearts and our spirits in ways which help us grow spiritually and personally in friendship with You and with those You place in our lives. Amen

October 20

REFLECTION

We are called to live in hope with eager expectation. What am I hoping for God to do or bring about in my life today?

PRAYER

Gracious God, direct our hearts and our attitudes to live with hope and trust in Your goodness and in the goodness of others around us… family, friends, co-workers, and all we serve. Open our eyes to see the beauty and goodness as they are revealed. Amen

October 21

REFLECTION

God invites us every day to serve and witness in a unique and meaningful way. What may God be calling me to do or to be for another person today?

PRAYER

Ever-Present God, help us to be attuned to the ways You call each of us to serve others and witness to the love and compassion You desire to be shared among us. Make us instruments of Your peace this day. Amen

October 22

REFLECTION

They are closest to us who best understand what life means to us, who can feel as we feel, and are able to stand with us in triumph and disaster, helping to lift us from a sense of feeling alone. Who are the persons in my life who stand with me in times of joy and in times of struggle?

PRAYER

God, thank You for being always present and available to us, as we journey through life. Thank You for those persons who understand what we value in life and who stand with us when times are good, and in times of darkness. Amen

October 23

REFLECTION

Our actions reflect what is in our hearts. What will my actions, words, and behaviors reflect today?

PRAYER

All-Knowing God, make what is in my heart pure and true. Direct my words, actions, and behaviors each day so that I may reflect the goodness, comfort, and encouragement which someone I meet may need this day. Amen

October 24

REFLECTION

Peace is not gained by holding tightly to our own needs and opinions, but by having open minds and hearts to seek out understanding and connections. In what ways am I open to seek understanding, truth and wisdom from those around me?

PRAYER

Eternal God, guide us in Your ways which bring understanding and peace among us. Let us always seek what is right and good for those we serve and live among each day. Amen

October 25

REFLECTION

Compassion is not the same as pity. Pity suggests distance, even a certain condescendence toward another. As I relate with others in their suffering or time of need, what do they experience in me… compassion or pity?

PRAYER

Loving God, create in me a heart of true compassion for those I meet each day. Help me to see as You see, to understand as You understand, and to reflect Your compassion and tenderness in my life. Amen

October 26

REFLECTION

Compassion involves letting ourselves come close to the one who suffers. To do this we need to be willing to become vulnerable ourselves…to acknowledge our own human limitations and feelings. How often do I reflect on my own human limitations and vulnerabilities?

PRAYER

God of Compassion, You made Yourself vulnerable as You emptied Yourself and came to live among us on this earth. Show us how to walk closely with our brothers and sisters who suffer and need our compassionate, understanding care. Amen

October 27

REFLECTION

The life of a compassionate person reveals: I am you brother; I am your sister; I am human, fragile, and limited, just like you. I do not see your tears as weakness, nor am I afraid to be with you in your pain. I too have wept. I too have felt deep human pain. We can only draw close and be with a person when they cease to be the "other" and are seen as one like us. Am I able to truly feel with another in their time of suffering and pain?

God of Humility and Truth, You have drawn near to experience our pain, our weakness, our human limitations and frailty. Teach us how to do this for one another, so that Your compassion and mercy may be reflected in all we do. Amen

October 28

REFLECTION

We know that kindness will not heal all wounds, nor will it solve every problem or disagreement. Yet every act of kindness is an extension of God's grace given to us freely, and something we can pass on to others. Do I serve with a true spirit of kindness?

PRAYER

Gracious God, help me to be generous in offering kindness to everyone I meet today. Help me to be aware that what may seem small or insignificant to me might be what is needed to help another person survive a difficult day. Amen

October 29

REFLECTION

For some people being negative may seem easier than being positive. There could be a downside to something good, or a hurdle to something desirable. The challenge comes in finding the good in what we have, the opportunity in every hurdle, and the positive in the difficult. Do I usually work from a negative or from a positive position in life?

PRAYER

God of Hope, transform our vision and our attitudes that we might find the good and the positive in each situation we encounter, and in each person You bring into our lives this day. Complete the good work You have begun in each of us. Amen

October 30

REFLECTION

There comes that mysterious and sacred encounter in life when someone acknowledges who we are and what we can be, igniting the fire of our highest potential for good. Who has acknowledged the inner beauty and potential of who I am and what I can be in my life?

PRAYER

God our Creator, thank You for creating within each of us the sacredness and potential to grow and become the best You have made us to be. Help us to affirm and encourage the goodness and potential in one another, so as to build up the common good for all. Amen

October 31

REFLECTION

The person who is trustworthy in small matters is also trustworthy in great ones; and the person who is dishonest in small matters is also dishonest in great ones. *(Luke 16:10)* What might be the measure of my integrity today?

PRAYER

Generous God, guide us to be honest and true stewards of all You entrust to us each day. In small matters and in greater matters, may our actions and decisions reveal the trustworthy character of our lives. Amen

November

November 1

REFLECTION

Who are the "saints" among us today? Perhaps they are the ones who live in the awareness that all they have is blessing and gift. They experience and give thanks for the unconditional love and mercy of God. They give themselves unselfishly in humble service to all God's people with love and compassion. They reflect the goodness of God in human form.

PRAYER

Holy God, teach us to deepen and reflect in our lives the love, mercy, and humble service You call us to extend to one another. Help us to live in the awareness that all we have are Your gifts and blessings to be enjoyed and shared with others with a generous spirit Amen

November 2

REFLECTION

Remember that when you leave this earth, you take with you nothing that you have received…only what you have given: a full heart, enriched by honest service, love, sacrifice, and courage. *(St. Francis of Assisi)* What will be my legacy and the gift of my life given to others when I die?

PRAYER

God, renew in us a faithful and generous spirit. Continually move us to greater love and service of one another. Amen

November 3

REFLECTION

God is not disturbed by differences, for it is God who created the variety and differences we experience in life all around us. Have I grown to appreciate the variety and differences I experience in life and in those I work with and serve, or am I usually just disturbed by them?

PRAYER

God of all creation, You create in each of us a beauty and uniqueness all its own. Thank You for the wonder and variety You have created in nature and the universe around us. Give us the vision to appreciate and reverence all You have made. Amen

November 4

REFLECTION

Those who trust in God shall understand truth, and the faithful shall live with God in love. *(Wisdom 3:9)* What new understanding or deeper truth have I come to know because I trusted God in times of uncertainty?

PRAYER

God of Truth and Wisdom, guide our hearts in times of uncertainty to trust in Your guidance and care. Teach us the deeper truths and meaning of life as we seek to grow in faithfulness and love. Amen

November 5

REFLECTION

Be aware of the miracles in life around you today. What will I see and count as miracles and blessings in my life or the life of others today?

Gracious God, You bring into our lives many miracles and blessings, great and small. Open our eyes and our awareness to see these and to live with grateful and joyful hearts. Amen

November 6

REFLECTION

Not only bread, but all things necessary for life are given on loan to us with others, and because of others, and for others, and to others through us. *(Meister Eckhart)* Do I tend to hold with open hands, or with clutching hands, all the gifts of life I have been given?

PRAYER

Generous and Giving God, remind us again today that all we have come to us as Your gifts. Teach us generosity of spirit as we open our hands and our hearts to share what we have with those around us, especially those who are most in need. Amen

November 7

REFLECTION

Many times a small gift of kindness, understanding, or being present with another, brings abundant unexpected rewards. What small gift will I give to another today that may enrich their life and perhaps also my own?

PRAYER

God of the small and the ordinary things in life, guide us today to gift others with our kindness, understanding, and reassuring presence in their time of need. May our lives reflect how You are ever and always God-with-us. Amen

November 8

REFLECTION

Put on a heart of compassion, kindness, humility, gentleness, and patience, bearing with one another and forgiving one another. *(Colossians 3:12)* People may not remember my words today, but they will remember how they felt when they were with me. How will others experience by behavior and attitude today?

PRAYER

God of Wisdom, direct not only our minds today, but also our hearts so that our interactions with others touch them with true kindness and reverence. Amen

November 9

REFLECTION

If we can let go of measuring what we've given or received, we can become truly free to do what is generous and loving for its own sake and the benefit of those we serve. Do I give and serve without expectations or conditions attached?

PRAYER

Generous God, soften and free our hearts to be true servants and Your instruments in the healing ministry You have entrusted to us. Amen

November 10

REFLECTION

Could this be one way of saying what our purpose on earth might be: To give my whole self, attention, good cheer, and desire to do what is right and good into the stream of life for the service of others? What purpose in life helps me to get up each morning and move into my day?

Creator God, as I move into my day and reflect on my life, guide me to see and give thanks for the purpose and meaning of this precious gift of life You have given to me. Amen

November 11
A Prayer for Veterans Day

Loving God, we ask Your blessings on all those who have served our country in branches of the military. We ask Your healing for our Veterans and their families who have been wounded, in body and spirit, in conflicts around our world. Bring comfort and honor to each of them. We ask for an end to wars and the dawning of an era of peace, as a way to honor all Veterans who have served in past and present wars. Bring peace to the hearts of our Veterans and peace to the regions of the world where they served. Protect all who serve in places of danger and in non-combative areas as well; may their call to service continue in their lives in many positive ways.

Give us all the creative vision to see a world which, grown weary with fighting, moves to affirming the life and dignity of every human being as precious and good, created by You, so we can move beyond fear, conflict and war. Hear our prayer, O Prince of Peace, and give us peace, Your true and lasting peace. Amen

November 12

Many persons, who had the opportunity to be in the presence of Jesus, found in him a fresh invitation to be in touch with God. Hurt by past judgments that set them apart, they found in Jesus the experience of God's compassionate love for them. What will others feel as they are in my presence today?

PRAYER

Indwelling God, I pray that Your presence within me will be a gift of comfort, acceptance, and hope made visible and felt by all I interact with today. Amen

November 13

REFLECTION

When we are confronted with difficult news or medical prognosis, we naturally can be filled with emotions like fear, disappointment, uncertainty, and anger. In times like this, how does my faith and relationship with God sustain me?

PRAYER

God of Strength, grant each of us the courage, faith, strength and comfort we need to make it through the times of darkness and uncertainty in our lives. Help us always trust in Your care and presence in our lives. Amen

November 14

REFLECTION

If we live our lives remembering that all our actions are known in the presence of God, we will live more truly with integrity, kindness, and compassion. What do my actions and behaviors reflect and reveal each day?

PRAYER

Ever-Present God, transform our hearts and our actions a little more each day that we may live with inner integrity, with kindness and compassion in all that we do. Amen

November 15

REFLECTION

When a blind man cried out to Jesus as he walked along the road, Jesus asked him, "What do you want me to do for you?" The blind man replied, "Lord, please let me see." *(Luke 18:40-41)* If God asked me, "What do you want me to do for you?" What would I ask for today?

PRAYER

God, our Faithful Companion, as we walk along the road of life each day, You are with us. Help us to be thoughtful and discerning in knowing when to ask for Your guidance and Your gifts to enrich our own lives and the lives of those we serve. Amen

November 16

REFLECTION

In order to get respect from your team, you have to give respect to each person involved. The true measure of a person is how they treat someone who may have little to give them in return. How do I treat each person I work with or interact with each day?

PRAYER

Gracious God, guide us to treat each person we encounter or work with today with the kind of respect and consideration we would want for ourselves. Open our eyes to see the inner goodness and worth of all persons we meet. Amen

November 17

REFLECTION

When asked if death is the final step, Sir Walter Scott replied, "No it is the final awakening." As I awake to begin my day, do I give thanks for the gift of another day, with opportunities to accomplish something worthwhile, or to help make life better for another person?

Loving God, thank You for the blessings of peaceful rest and sleep. Thank You for the opportunities for good which each new day brings into our lives. Amen

November 18

REFLECTION

For every one of us that succeeds, there is someone who has shown us the way. Who has shown me the way and been an encouraging mentor in my life?

PRAYER

Shepherding God, continue to lead, guide, and encourage us as we use our skills and knowledge each day to serve Your people in need. Thank You for those You have placed in our lives who have shown us the way and been good mentors for us. Amen

November 19

REFLECTION

Right now you may be one choice away from making a new beginning. Choices are like habits; they can be our worst enemy or our best friend. What thoughtful, intentional choices will I make today?

PRAYER

Creator God, You place before us each day the opportunity of making choices which will affect our lives and the lives of those around us. Guide us to make wise and good choices which reflect the good You desire for each of us. Amen

November 20

REFLECTION

Those who have achieved success are the ones who have lived well, laughed often, and loved much. They are the ones who leave the world better than they found it. Their lives become an inspiration to those who have known them. Who are the persons I have observed who live with this spirit?

PRAYER

Life-Giving God, guide us each day so that all we do will make the world around us a better place than we found it. Thank You for those who inspire us to live well, laugh often, and love much every day. Amen

November 21

REFLECTION

Your vision will become clear only when you look into your heart … the one who looks outside, dreams. The one who looks inside, awakens. *(Carl Jung)* What do I do to seek clear vision, understanding and direction in my life?

PRAYER

Redeeming God, guide us to pause in our day and at important times in our life's journey to look inside, to awaken, to find clear vision, understanding, and direction in our lives. May what we find help us to serve You and Your people well each day. Amen

November 22

REFLECTION

In the middle of every difficulty lies opportunity. *(Albert Einstein)* What are the difficulties I face today, and what might be the opportunities for good that come with them?

All Providing God, be with us as we face the difficulties which may come our way today. Guide us and direct us with wisdom to know how to handle these and also to find the opportunities for good which they offer as well. Amen

November 23

REFLECTION

We can let the circumstances of our lives harden us so that we become increasingly resentful and afraid, or we can let them soften us, and make us kinder. The choice is up to us. How do I let the events and circumstances of my life shape and form me?

PRAYER

Faithful God, You walk the journey of life with us each day. Protect and shield us from what may be harmful to us and those we love. Guide us to let the events of each day soften us and make us more kind as we serve in Your name. Amen

November 24

REFLECTION

If there were one word that could act as a standard of conduct for one's entire life, perhaps it would be 'thoughtfulness.' *(Confucius)* How thoughtful am I in my daily life…toward the needs of others, in knowing and choosing to do what is truly right and good?

PRAYER

Gracious God, You choose each day to be always thoughtful in caring and providing for us. Teach us how to grow in our own thoughtfulness, that we may see the needs of others and respond to them with generosity and kindness. Amen

November 25

REFLECTION

In all things, give thanks. Let gratitude be the light and energy which guides and directs you from within. What blessings am I most grateful for in my life at this time? What blessings do I sometimes take for granted?

PRAYER

Gracious and Loving Creator, thank You for the freedoms we enjoy in our nation. Thank you for the blessings of faith, family, health, shelter and food which we enjoy. Guide us to always live with grateful hearts and to share our blessings with others in need. Amen

November 26

REFLECTION

Listening is the fundamental attitude and posture needed in our times of prayer. In my own times of prayer, do I tend to speak and use a lot of words, or do I also spend time in quiet and listening?

PRAYER

Ever-Present God, guide us in our relationship with You to take time during our day and week for moments of quiet, reflection, and listening. In our prayer, may we listen as well as speak our words of praise, thanks, or express our needs to You. Amen

November 27

REFLECTION

Acts of kindness are simply the result of living by the Golden Rule. *(Sir Winston Churchill)* How well do I live the Golden Rule, 'Treat others the way you would like to be treated', in my daily life and interactions with others?

God of Compassion, as we live our lives each day, remind us to live the Golden Rule which comes to us in the Gospel message. May acts of kindness, courtesy, and consideration for others be a part of who we are everyday. Amen

November 28

REFLECTION

The Scriptures of the Advent Season invite us to look forward (to the end times), to look back (to the Bethlehem story), and to look within (our own hearts and lives) to discover in all of these that God is with us. As I reflect on the future, the Gospel stories, and my own life experiences, when and how do I find that God is with us?

PRAYER

Ever-Present God, teach us how to pray, reflect, and keep vigil in our lives, so that You, as God-with-us, may be born anew in our lives and in our world each day. Amen

November 29

REFLECTION

Holiness may not consist so much in extraordinary actions, but rather in living well our relationships with God, self, and others every day. How well do I live and grow in my relationship with God, others and myself each day?

PRAYER

Faithful God, direct my heart and my actions each day to live well my relationship with You and all those around me, as I seek to live and grow in holiness. Amen

November 30

REFLECTION

When God's Chosen One comes, the Spirit of the Lord is present, a Spirit of Wisdom, of Counsel, Understanding, of Strength, of Knowledge, and of Awe in God's presence. In what ways do I see the Spirit of the Lord present with others around me in my life and work?

PRAYER

Spirit of the Living God, fall afresh on us. Be present within and among us with Wisdom, good Counsel, Understanding, Strength, Knowledge, and Awe in Your presence as we live and serve each day. Amen

December

December 1

REFLECTION

It's the nature of our soul that often determines how we make our journey in life, not necessarily the calm or the strife which life presents. What is the nature of my soul today?

PRAYER

Faithful God, open my vision and my awareness to recognize what the nature of my soul is today. Give me peace and wisdom as I walk my journey in the midst of the calm and the strife which life presents. Amen

December 2

REFLECTION

Build your life on a firm foundation. Then when the rains, the floods, and the winds of life come, your life will not collapse or fall. You will be set solidly on the rock of your foundation. *(Matthew 7:24-27)* What is the foundation and solid rock I build my life upon?

PRAYER

Rock of Ages, our Firm Foundation, be our source of strength, comfort, and light when the rains, floods, and winds of life come. Sustain us and guide us in all we do each day. May we live and serve grounded in our relationship with You. Amen

December 3

REFLECTION

We are all meant to shine. We are born to make manifest the glory of God that is within us. It's not just in some of us, it's in everyone. As we let our light shine, we unconsciously give other people permission to do the same. As we are liberated from our own fears, our presence may also liberate others. In what ways will I let God's light shine in me today?

PRAYER

God of Light and Goodness, renew and enkindle Your light within each of us. Liberate us from any fears or barriers which may be preventing us from allowing Your goodness, compassion, and light from being fully present in us. Amen

December 4

REFLECTION

What greater thing is there than that God chose to become human and live among us, to reveal God's love and show us the way to live? How has God's human presence among us in time and history influenced and inspired my life?

PRAYER

Incarnate and Ever-Present God, thank You for choosing to be born in our own human likeness, living among us for a time on earth, revealing God's love and care for us, and showing us how to live with care and service of those around us each day. Renew this in us each day. Amen

December 5

REFLECTION

Prepare the way of the Lord, make straight his paths. Every valley shall be filled and every mountain and hill shall be made low. The winding roads shall be made straight, and the rough ways made smooth, and all shall see the salvation of our God. *(Luke 3:4-6)* Are there any barriers, rough ways or paths, which I need to attend to at this time in my life, so that the saving presence of God can be more present for me and for all those I interact with each day?

PRAYER

God of mercy, prepare in me the way for Your coming in our lives during this Advent Season. Guide us to remove the things which hinder us from open pathways to You and to one another. Come and bring us wisdom and peace. Amen

December 6
St. Nicholas Day

REFLECTION

Nicholas was a bishop who lived in the 3rd Century. He was known as one who generously shared his own resources and blessings anonymously with persons who were poor and in special need. His spirit of giving as "Santa Nicholas" has come down to us through the centuries in the well-known present figure of "Santa Claus", made famous in the poem "T'was the Night Before Christmas". In celebrating this day, many families have fun with the custom of hanging stockings on the night of December 5th, in hopes that good St. Nick will visit and leave a special treat of candy or fruit. What are some of the simple customs of Advent and Christmas you enjoy with your family and friends?

God of surprises, refresh our lives during this season as we celebrate customs and traditions with our family and friends. Give us a spirit of generosity and thoughtfulness as seen in the life of good St. Nick. Amen.

December 7

REFLECTION

Come to me, all you who labor and are burdened, and I will give you rest. *(Matthew 11:28)* Do you feel burdened or overwhelmed in any way with the activities and expectations of this busy holiday season? What can you do to slow the pace and enjoy the days more?

PRAYER

Merciful and Loving God, help us to keep the true focus and purpose of the Advent and Christmas Season in our hearts and in our lives. Help us to find ways to slow the pace and reflect on Your coming into our lives each day. Amen

December 8

REFLECTION

Each year on this day, we celebrate in prayer and reflection the call of Mary. Mary was chosen by God to be the mother of Jesus, the Son of God and our Savior. *(Luke 1:26-35)* Today we remember and celebrate Mary's openness, her generosity, her faith and trust in God's plan for her and all of humanity. When and how do I experience God's call in my own life? How do I respond to God's call each day?

PRAYER

God of miracles, just as You called Mary to carry Your Son Jesus within her and give birth to Him on this earth, touch our hearts to be open to Your call in our own lives. May we also carry the presence of Jesus within us, and see Him present in all those around us each day. May Christ be born anew in each of our lives this Christmas. Amen

December 9

REFLECTION

Let our lives be honest and holy in this present age, as we wait for the happiness to come when our great God is revealed in glory. *(Titus 2:12-13)* What can I do to keep my life honest and holy, so that I might recognize God's presence each day?

PRAYER

Ever-Present God, You reveal Yourself in so many ways each moment of our lives. Heal our blindness and refresh our awareness that we may see Your presence and actions in the events and persons we encounter each day. Amen

December 10

REFLECTION

I, the Lord, your God, will teach you what is for your good, and lead you on the way you should go. *(Isaiah 48:17)* How often do I take time for quiet and solitude in my life, to truly listen and become aware of God's guidance and direction in my life?

PRAYER

God of Wisdom, I desire to know all that is for my good and the good of those I love and care for. Make me more aware each day of how it is that I can follow in Your ways and know Your guidance in my life. Amen

December 11

REFLECTION

If you want God to hear your prayers, hear the voice of the poor. If you wish God to anticipate your needs, provide for the needs of those around you without waiting for them to ask you. In what ways will I notice and provide for the needs of others today before they have to ask?

Ever Attentive God, open our eyes and our hearts each day to generously notice and serve the needs of our co-workers and all who come to us in our lives and ministry. Amen

December 12

REFLECTION

Rejoice in the Lord always. Your kindness should be known to all. The Lord is near. May the peace of God, that surpasses all understanding, guard your hearts and minds in Christ Jesus. *(Philippians 4:4-7)* Does my life express joy, kindness and peace as I live and work with others each day?

PRAYER

Emmanuel, God-with-us, bring peace, kindness, joy and understanding to our lives in this Advent and Christmas Season. Through our interactions with others each day, may Your presence and nearness be revealed. Amen

December 13

REFLECTION

Where there is no love, put love and there you will find love. *(St. John of the Cross)* Where and how will I be called to bring love today?

PRAYER

God of Love, open our eyes and hearts today to see how we are called to bring love and kindness to others. Open our eyes and hearts to see when others are also bringing Your love and kindness to us. Amen

December 14

REFLECTION

The happiest people don't necessarily have the best of everything. They just make the most of everything that comes along their way. How will I live and serve today? What brings true happiness in my life?

PRAYER

God, Faithful Companion, continue to walk closely with us each day. Give us the peace, courage, and wisdom to make the most of what comes to us in the events, people, and situations of our day. Amen

December 15

REFLECTION

Faith is the main ingredient that combats fear. As long as our faith is bigger than our fears, we will always triumph. What usually seems to direct my life, my decisions, my behaviors… is it my fears or my faith?

PRAYER

Life-giving God, increase our faith and dispel our fears. May we trust in Your guidance in all that we do. Amen

December 16

REFLECTION

When we choose not to focus on what's missing in our lives, but are grateful for the abundance that is present, we may find a bit of heaven on earth. What do I tend to focus on in my life… what I don't have or all the blessings which I do have every day?

PRAYER

Gracious God, thank You for the over-flowing abundance of blessings and care which You share with us each day. Help us to not miss all the good that is before us because we focus on what we think is missing. Amen

December 17

REFLECTION

As God invites us into a closer relationship, God never seems to force anything on us. This conveys the amazing humility of God. We are always left with a choice about believing in and responding to God. What will I choose today?

PRAYER

Trusting and Patient God, I am humbled by Your daily invitation to grow in a closer relationship with You. Deepen my faith and my understanding of how to respond to Your call and love in my life. Amen

December 18

REFLECTION

An angel of the Lord appeared to Joseph in a dream and gave him guidance during a confusing time in his life. *(Matthew 1:18-25)* In some cultures dreams are regularly discussed over breakfast in order to learn and gain insight. How attentive am I to the subtle "nudges" or messages of God in my life? Do I act on them with trust?

PRAYER

Ever-Present God, open me to recognize all the ways You come to reveal Yourself, Your guidance and messages in my life. Help me to trust in Your word, Your love for me, and walk in Your ways. Amen

December 19

REFLECTION

In the Advent and Christmas Scriptures, we see that God arranged for the Messiah, the Savior, Jesus to come from a small and insignificant clan and town. How and when have I observed God acting and speaking through persons whom I would not have expected or looked to initially?

PRAYER

God of Surprises, You continue to come to us and communicate to us in unexpected ways. Touch our hearts, our eyes, and our ears that we will be open to recognize and accept all the ways You come to us and speak to us in our times. Amen

December 20

REFLECTION

Wonderful and beautiful things can happen when we are willing to hold lightly what God has given to us. As we pray, it is good to entrust both our prayer and the answer to God, who sees the bigger picture of life.

PRAYER

Faithful God, teach us to hold lightly and with open hands all that You have given to us. Give us the trust and confidence to know that You always desire what is good and ultimately life-giving for each of us. Amen

December 21

REFLECTION

Your ways, O Lord, make known to me; teach me your paths. *(Psalm 25:4)* God's ways are not always our ways. God's ways are not always clear or obvious to us either. How do I usually seek to know God's ways in my life? In the quiet of prayer… in Scripture… in conversation with a trusted friend or spiritual guide?

PRAYER

God of Wisdom, please make known to us Your ways each day—whether through Scripture, other people, or the movements of our own hearts. Amen

December 22

REFLECTION

I stand at the door and knock, says the Lord. If anyone hears my voice and opens the door, I will come in and sit down at table with them. *(Revelation 3:20)* Who might be standing at the door knocking or calling out to me in this Christmas Season? Will I open the door of my heart and my life to receive and welcome them?

PRAYER

Emmanuel, God-with-us, open our awareness and our hearts so that we listen and open ourselves to the unanticipated ways You may come to us in this Christmas Season and throughout the coming New Year. Amen

December 23

REFLECTION

In the Hebrew Scriptures, Isaiah envisioned a time of great joy when the Promised One comes. *(Isaiah 9:1-6)* What special joy have I experienced as I prepare for Christmas and celebrate this time with friends, family, and faith communities?

PRAYER

With the angels in the Gospel of Luke, we sing and pray, Glory to God in the highest and on earth peace to all on whom God's favor rests. Loving God, let Your favor and Your peace rest upon each of us this day and always. Amen

December 24

REFLECTION

A light has shown in our darkness. Our God has come to live among us to show us the way. A Child is born to us, and they name him Wonder-Counselor, God-Hero, Father-Forever, Prince of Peace. What is the special "light" or gift of Christmas that shines in my life this Holy Season?

PRAYER

Jesus, our Light, help us to see You even more clearly in the events and persons in our lives this Christmas. Thank You for humbling Yourself to come and be God-with-us each day we live. Amen

December 25
Christmas Day

REFLECTION

The Christmas story is filled with surprises. God comes to earth not as a full-grown, powerful king, but as a vulnerable newborn baby. He is born not in a palace, but in a simple stable with straw and animals. He is born to a poor, humble young couple. His first visitors were shepherds from a nearby field. How open am I to the God of Surprises? Can I let go of my own expectations and preconceived ideas, so that I can truly see God present in the unexpected events of my life?

PRAYER

God of Surprises, help me to be more open to the amazing things You are doing in my life and in our world this Christmas Day. Help me to see every day as a gift from You, and rejoice in Your coming in the events and persons I encounter. Amen

December 26

REFLECTION

Small truths can be expressed in words. Great and deeper truths can only be pondered in silence and awe. What are the deeper truths and mysteries of this Christmas Season which I ponder in silence and awe?

PRAYER

Incarnate God-with us, thank You for the wondrous gift of presence You shared as You chose to live and walk among us on this earth. Continue to teach us Your ways of peace, compassion, and love as we share our lives with one another. Amen

December 27

REFLECTION

As we continue to celebrate in this Christmas Season, where do I find God-with-us in the persons and events of my day and my life? Am I too busy, or maybe even blind, to notice how God is new and fresh in my life each day?

PRAYER

Emmanuel, You came to dwell among us not only more than 2000 years ago in Bethlehem, but You come again in our own time every day. Open our eyes so that we may recognize and welcome You in the persons and events of our day, as well as in the inner stillness of our own lives. Amen

December 28

REFLECTION

The magical stardust of Christmas glistens on the faces of believers ever so briefly, reminding us of what is worth having and what we are intended to be. Am I still enjoying the magical stardust of Christmas in my life, and reflecting on what is truly worth having and sharing?

PRAYER

All Powerful, yet unseen God, the coming of Your light into our world has refreshed and renewed us again. Guide us to live and rejoice in the spirit of Christmas through the end of this year and into the New Year. Amen

December 29

REFLECTION

Fill the lives of others with sweetness. Speak kindly to others with encouraging words, while their ears can hear them and while their hearts can be affirmed. Do my words and interactions with others bring sweetness and hope?

PRAYER

Gracious God, thank You for all the ways You lift us up each day and provide for our needs. Help our words and kindness for others to be genuine and life-giving, for we do not know the burdens or concerns which others carry in their hearts each day. Amen

December 30

REFLECTION

The last temptation is the greatest treason: to do the right thing for the wrong reason. *(T.S. Eliot)* What are my motives as I seek to do what is right… for show… to impress someone… to get something in return…or just because it is the right and good thing to do?

PRAYER

God of all times and seasons, guide us as we prepare for this year to end and a new year to begin. Help us to take some time to reflect on the direction our lives are going and the choices we are making. Help us to always do what is right and good in Your sight. Amen

December 31

REFLECTION

There is a difference between knowledge and wisdom. One helps you make a living, the other helps you make a life. What wisdom have I acquired through the events and life-situations I have experienced in this year about to end?

PRAYER

Gracious God, as we come to the end of this year of grace You have given to each of us, guide us to take time for a life review. May the good we have done and the wisdom we have gained bring glory to You and a growing maturity to our own lives. Amen

Section II
Other Prayer Resources
for Individual or Group Use

Prayers for Other Times
Along Life's Journey

Monthly Gathering Prayers for Meetings

Letting God Speak to Us
in Times of Anxiety or Illness

Prayers for Other Times
Along Life's Journey

A Mother's Prayer During Pregnancy

Loving God, Creator of all life,
I know You are with me
and with my baby growing within me
during this special time of pregnancy.
I thank You for blessing my husband and me
with the privilege of being co-creators with You
in giving life to this precious child yet to be born.
What an awesome and sacred experience
this is to feel our baby moving and growing
within me with each new day!
Please help me to have a safe delivery
and a healthy baby when the time
of giving birth comes.
Gracious and Loving God,
be with me now and each day to come
as I place my trust in You.
Amen

A Prayer before Surgery

O Healing God,
the hours seem so long in my time of waiting.
I feel restless, and there are so many thoughts
going through my mind;
thoughts about the outcome of my surgery,
about my future, about my family.
I feel fear and anxiety because it's my own body,
my own life that is so vulnerable at this time.
I raise my voice to You, O God,
asking that You may replace my fears with trust.
Replace my anxiety with faith in Your healing
human instruments whom You will guide.
Bless the doctors and medical staff
who will be involved with my surgery.
Guide their hands to bring healing
where there is injury or disease,
and strength where there is weakness.
Bless my family and friends
who, through their presence and support,
have given me strength and courage to face this moment.
Bless my time of waiting.
Help me rest peacefully in Your loving protection,
so that I will be ready for my surgery tomorrow.
Amen.

A Prayer for the Healers

Faithful God, You are the source of strength
and hope in our lives.
Bless this hospital where I find myself,
that it may be a place of healing and compassion.
Bless the people whom You have chosen to be instruments
of Your healing, that they may be humble
and knowledgeable channels of Your grace.
Where there is danger, may they protect life;
where there is weakness and pain,
may they provide relief and comfort;
where there is anxiety and fear,
may they offer gentle reassurances through
their presence and kindness;
and where all human efforts fail,
may they be assured that we can rest secure in You.
Bless all who work in this hospital
with a gentle and compassionate heart,
that they may find the way
to live and model Your goodness.
Bless me too, so that through this experience,
I may strengthen my faith in You
and gain a deeper understanding in my life.
Amen

A Prayer in Time of Illness

Good and Gracious God,
send Your peace and blessing upon me
to sustain me and give me strength.
Every day You show your care for Your creation
by nourishing all that You have made.
Enable me, one whom You have created,
to recognize Your loving presence
whenever You reach out to me in Your word,
in Your people, and in the mystery of my life.
As I am now experiencing this illness,
I pray that You will bless the doctors,
the nurses, the chaplains, and all
to whom You have entrusted Your
ministry of healing.
Help my body, mind, and spirit to be
receptive to Your healing so that
I may receive strength and courage
in times of anxiety and fear,
and renewed health through Your healing power.
Amen

A Prayer for Trust

O God of the journey,
help me believe that behind the clouds
there is the sun, even when it rains.
Help me believe that barren trees of winter
will bear new leaves again,
if I am patient enough to wait.
Help me realize the only way to reach a mountain
may be to walk through the long valley;
the only way a candle can share its light
is by gradually dying to itself.
God, help me to let go of the securities
that make me insecure;
teach me to let go of the fears
that make me restless and anxious.
Yes, I am afraid because I am so used
to being in control. I don't like to feel vulnerable.
I get edgy when things don't go as I had planned.
I place myself in Your loving care,
just as a child who feels secure in a parent's arms.
Help me to trust that You will give me strength
and see me through all that life may bring.
Amen

A Prayer in Time of Uncertainty

O God, My Rock and my Stronghold,
It is in times like this when I experience my own
human limitations, the weakness of my body,
the uncertainty of the future, and I turn to You in prayer.
I ask not for a miracle, but for patience;
not for freedom from suffering,
but for the strength to bear it.
Help me, O God, to rest in quiet and trust
when words cannot express what I feel.
Please come and ease my fears and anxieties
as I open myself to fuller trust in You.
Let the reassuring words You offered Your disciples
be mine today: "Be not afraid for I am with you always
until the end of time." "Be not afraid for I am with you,"
no matter what may come.
Help me remember that both joy and suffering
are a part of our human condition.
Please let me feel and know that You are with me,
holding me close with Your reassuring presence
and Your loving care at this time.
Amen

A Prayer for Persons Sick or Injured

Compassionate and Healing God,
we pray today for all
who are sick or injured.
Let Your hand of healing
and protection be upon them.
Ease any fears or anxieties
they may be experiencing.
Let them feel Your comfort
and the comfort of those around them.
When they feel afraid,
give them strength and courage.
When they feel alone,
send them someone who can
listen and be present to them.
When they feel confused,
give them reassurance and direction.
When they are in pain,
provide them with caregivers
who can ease their suffering.
In their times of darkness,
help them to be sustained
by the resources of their faith
and inner spirit.
May all who are sick or injured
know You are with them today
and You hold them always
in Your loving embrace.
Amen

The Caregiver's Prayer

Compassionate and Healing God,
help us to see Your face
in the faces of our brothers and sisters
who are sick or injured.
Guide us to reach out to them
with hearts of compassion
and hands which serve their needs.
When they are anxious,
help us know how to reassure them.
When they feel alone,
help us notice and be present.
When they feel confused,
help us to listen and assist
in finding answers to their concerns.
When they need comfort,
help us communicate
care and understanding.
When they are weak or discouraged,
help us find ways to refresh their spirits.
When doubt or darkness touches them,
give Your light to guide them
and lift them up.
Help us as caregivers to always
turn to You as the Source
of our own strength and compassion,
as we seek to serve the needs
of our sisters and brothers
who are sick and vulnerable.
Amen

A Prayer for Healthcare Workers

Spirit of the Living God,
bless the work of our hands, our minds, and our hearts.
May the service we offer be a reflection
of all that is good within us.
In our planning, our creating, and our doing,
give us wisdom and insight to patiently listen
for the stirring of Your presence and Your guidance.
Grace us with a sense of inner peace in the midst of our daily
routines.
Enliven our spirits with joy as we serve Your people in need.
Fill us with reverence for others and gratitude for our diversity.
Touch our hearts with the awareness that our work is sacred.
May unity, beauty, truth, compassion, and healing be the fruit
of our labor each day as we serve together in Your name.
Amen

Morning Prayers

1.

Good Morning, Gracious God and Creator. I thank You for the gift of this new day. You invite all who are burdened in any way to come to You. Extend Your healing hand to touch me today. Touch my soul with Your compassion for others. Touch my heart with Your courage and infinite love for all. Touch my mind with Your wisdom, that my words may always proclaim Your praise. Teach me to reach out to You in my times of need, and help me to lead others to You by my example. Bring me health in body, mind, and spirit that I may serve You with all my strength. Touch gently this life which You have created today and every day I am blessed to live. Amen

2.

Loving God, make me an instrument of Your peace.
Where there is hatred, let me sow love.
Where there is injury, pardon.
Where there is doubt, faith.
Where there is despair, hope.
Where there is darkness, light.
Where there is sadness, joy.
Divine Master, grant that I may not so much seek to be
consoled, as to console. To be understood, as to understand.
To be loved, as to love. For it is in giving that we receive.
It is in pardoning that we are pardoned. And it is in dying
that we are born to eternal life. Amen
(Prayer of St. Francis of Assisi)

3.

Good morning, Faithful God. The night has passed and a new day has come. Once again I gaze upon Your world and find it good. The darkness fades, and new light has come. You are present to share this day, just as You watched with me through the night. I cannot see what lies ahead, but I am sure You know. So take my hand and walk with me wherever I go. Be with me in times of joy and in times of pain. I trust that You are here with me and will guide me along my way. In this awareness of Your loving care, I say, Good morning, Faithful God. Amen

4.

Thank You, God, for the gift of this new day. If I can do some good today, if I can serve along life's way, if I can help someone in need, God, show me the way. If I can right a human wrong, if I can help someone be strong, if I can lift someone with a smile or kind word, God, show me how. If I can aid someone in distress, if I can make a burden less, if I can spread more happiness today, God, please show me the way. Amen

Evening Prayers

1.

God of Love, as evening comes, teach me patience and trust. Quiet me to wait to hear Your counsel. So often I want to be beyond what is happening now, and hope for You to fulfill my plans. But now I wait, yearning for Your light to dispel the darkness I feel. I desire to know and embrace Your wisdom that always leads to wholeness and inner healing. Amen

2.

Saving God, as evening comes, I turn to You for comfort and reassurance in my time of illness and healing. You are the horizon beyond all that we know and see. You are the safety net that catches and holds me secure. Teach me the path of true humility, so that I can learn to share in Your strength and loving care. Amen

3.

Loving God, as evening comes, help me to look back and give thanks for the blessings of this day… the kindnesses shown me, the smiles, the care and compassion given me by those I have met and who have assisted me today. I recall these blessings now as I welcome the night and the rest I pray it will bring. Amen

4.

God of Compassion, as evening comes, I am grateful for the privilege of prayer. I'm grateful I can call out to You and know You are there even when life seems difficult or uncertain. I am grateful for the peace that comes to fill my soul, for the strength You give to me when my own strength seems to be spent or drained. I ask You to increase my faith and renew my hope so I may rest secure this night. Amen

A Prayer of Gratitude for our Mothers

REFLECTION

What women in your life have nurtured and given life to you... your mother, grandmother, aunt, sister, mentor, friend? Whether they are living now or have already gone before us, take time today to thank them and rejoice in their goodness.

PRAYER

God of Life, thank You for our mothers, grandmothers, and other women who have given us life and continue to nurture life within us. Bless all those we love with strong faith and good health, as we rejoice in Your gift of life today. Amen

A Prayer of Gratitude for our Fathers

REFLECTION

Who are the men in your life who have modeled what it is to be a good father, grandfather, husband, brother, mentor in life? What qualities, virtues, and strengths do they have and share with others?

PRAYER

Loving God, thank You today for our fathers, grandfathers and husbands, both living and deceased. Thank you for the blessing they have been and continue to be in our lives. Bless each of them today with what they need to serve their families and model the goodness which reflects Your presence among us. Amen

Monthly Gathering Prayers

Gathering Prayer for January

God of all times and seasons, thank You for the gift
of this New Year.

As we open ourselves to the blessings
You have in store for each of us,
give us grateful and generous hearts.

Guide us in this New Year to use
the skills and abilities You have given us
to serve others with compassion and loving care.

As doors of new opportunities and challenges
open to us this year,
help us to trust in and feel Your presence with us.

Inspire and direct us to always do what is right and good.

Help us to find ways to support and encourage one another
as we work together to create the best experience
for all we serve and work among.

Open us to see You present in all those around us,
to draw forth and celebrate their life and goodness,
to lift up and not tear down,
to bring hope and support in times of struggle.

May the Light and Peace You have shared with us
be the gift we can give to others in this new year. Amen

1. As this New Year begins, what new opportunities and new beginnings do I look forward to embracing in my life this year?
2. What can I do this year that will help bring hope, support, and
encouragement to my family, my co-workers and those we serve?

Gathering Prayer for February

Loving God, as we pray and work together this month,
the symbol of the human heart often appears before us.

We celebrate American Heart Month,
we celebrate Valentine Day,
and we desire to renew our own hearts and spirits
as we seek to serve You and Your people in need.

Guide us to have healthy and generous hearts.

Free our hearts of judging others and open us
to see You present in all those we serve.

Dispel any darkness in our hearts
and permeate us with Your light.

Cleanse our hearts of any bitterness or resentment
and refresh us with forgiveness.

Free our hearts of any self-serving attitudes
and fill us with empathy and understanding toward others.

Empty our hearts of discontent
and recharge us with thankfulness.

Release any anxiety in our hearts and fill us with hope.

Amen

1. In what ways do my attitudes and behaviors lift the hearts of others?
2. What could I do this month to make my "heart" lighter and healthier?

Gathering Prayer for March

Creating and Life-Giving God,
we welcome the coming of Spring
and seek to renew our own inner spirits
in this month of March.

Open our eyes and our hearts to see and welcome
the ways You are calling each of us to new life
within ourselves and with each other.

Help us to be generous and gentle in planting the seeds
which will bring forth healing, new life,
and an abundance of true compassion
for all those we serve and interact with each day.

Give us patience with ourselves and others
as we nurture life and growth in each other through
the waters of kindness, the sunshine of encouragement,
and being rooted in the rich soil
of our faith-based ministry.

As we delight in the beauty and wonders
of Spring now unfolding,
renew our vision and continue to remind us of
all You call us to be, as we serve Your people in need.

Amen

1. What delights me and lifts my spirit in this Spring Season?
2. How might I need to be more patient with others and myself
   in order that new life and resurrection can come?

Gathering Prayer for April

Gracious God, thank You for creating and sharing with us
the wonders and beauty of this Spring and Easter Season!

You have made us co-creators in the process of Your creation.

You have blessed us with wisdom, reason, creativity,
talents and skills.

Guide us to use our skills in ways which bring about
healing, hope, and new life for all those we serve.

Help us learn from one another, for You have blessed each of us
with gifts to benefit the common good of all.

As flowers appear on the earth
and trees bring forth their blossoms,
let each of our lives bring forth kindness and patience,
compassion and care for our co-workers and those we serve.

Plant within each of us new seeds of joy, hope, and strength.

Help us to always stay focused on what is right and good,
in all we do and all we are called to be.

Bring new life to each of us in this season of resurrection.

Amen

1. What in nature delights my spirit and brings me hope and joy
   in this Spring Season?
2. What signs of new life, hope and care do I experience among
   our staff?

Gathering Prayer for May

Life-Giving God, during this month of May
we thank You for the abundance of new life and fresh colors
which we are enjoying in nature all around us.

This month we honor and celebrate the women
who have given us life
and those who continue to nurture life and hope in us…
our mothers, grandmothers, wives, sisters,
friends, and mentors.

Thank You for the blessings You have given to each of them,
and all the ways they share their goodness with us.

We ask Your blessings and healing touch for all women
whom you have called us to serve.

Help us to honor and reverence these women and their families
as we welcome and care for them each day.

Deepen in each of us a spirit of compassion, reverence and love
which reflects Your presence in all we do.

We ask this in Your name.

Amen

1. Who are the persons who nurture life, hope and encouragement in my life?
2. In what ways do I nurture life, hope and encouragement in the lives of others?

Gathering Prayer for June

Creator God, during this month of June
we thank You for the abundant blessings
of this summer season.

This month we honor and celebrate the men
who have given us life
and those who continue to nurture life and hope in us…
our fathers, grandfathers, husbands, brothers,
friends, and mentors.

Thank You for the blessings You have given to each of them,
and all the ways they share their goodness with us.

We ask Your blessings and healing touch for all men
whom you have called us to serve.

Help us to honor and reverence these men and their families
as we welcome and care for them each day.

Deepen in each of us a spirit of compassion,
skill and excellence
to bring Your presence and healing in all we do.

We ask this in Your name.

Amen

1. Who are the persons who have nurtured life, a healthy self-esteem and encouragement in my life?
2. In what ways do I show respect, care and encouragement toward others?

Gathering Prayer for July

Ever-Present God,
as we enjoy the gifts of these early Summer days
we give thanks to You for the miracles and wonders
of life which we see in nature all around us.

In Your faithfulness, You have brought forth again
an abundance of flowers and vegetation
in a marvelous array of rainbow colors
and fresh produce for all to enjoy.

May the work that we do in our lives and ministry
be in partnership with Your on-going creative love
for all we serve and work among.

May our hands bring Your healing touch,
our words bring Your voice of comfort,
our compassion and kindness reveal
that You are present among us guiding all we do.

Amen

1. What have I noticed as I walk outside or as I drive to work that reveal to me the abundance of God's goodness and faithfulness?
2. How do I experience God guiding my hands, my words, my actions as I work?

Gathering Prayer for August

Loving God, as employees of _____,
we are rooted in the loving ministry of Jesus
as teacher and healer.

We commit ourselves to serving all persons,
with special attention to those who are poor and vulnerable.

Help us to serve all persons who come to us
with kindness and compassion.

Guide us in our faith-based ministry as we strive
to be dedicated to spiritually centered, holistic care,
sustaining and improving the health and well-being
of individuals and communities.

Direct us to be advocates for a compassionate and just society
through our actions and words each day.

We ask this in your name.

Amen

1. In what ways do I experience what I do as part of a teaching and healing ministry?
2. In what ways do I offer "spiritually centered holistic care" to others?

Gathering Prayer for September

Gracious and Loving God,
thank You for the ministry of care which You have entrusted
to us as we serve together, welcoming persons who are ill,
injured, and poor who come to us each day.

Help us to care for all persons with kindness and compassion.
Open our eyes to recognize You in each person we meet,
especially those who are anxious, afraid, or alone.

Help us to treat each person as we would want to be treated
and as we would want our own family members to be treated.

Strengthen us in our own times of tiredness or discouragement.
Lift us up to always be the best we can be
and to live with grateful hearts each day.

Amen

1. What do I do to take care of my own health and gift of life, as I serve the needs of others at work and in my family?
2. In what ways do I support and encourage my co-workers, especially when they may be struggling, discouraged or carrying a heavy burden?

Gathering Prayer for October

Lord, make us instruments of Your peace.

Where there is hatred, let us bring love;
Where there is injury, let us bring pardon;
Where there is doubt, let us bring faith;
Where there is despair, let us bring hope;
Where there is darkness, let us bring light;
And where there is sadness, let us bring joy.

Grant that we not seek so much
To be consoled as to console,
To be understood, as to understand,
To be loved as to love.

For it is in giving that we receive,
It is in pardoning that we are pardoned,
And it is in dying that we are born to eternal life.

Amen

(Adapted Prayer of St. Francis of Assisi)

1. As I read this prayer, which line or phrase is most comforting to me?
2. As I read this prayer, which line or phrase is most challenging to me?
3. What can we do to help us live in the spirit of this prayer, as we work with each other and as we serve others each day?

Gathering Prayer for November

Gracious God,
give us thankful and generous hearts,
to share the gifts and blessings You have given to each of us.

May we always acknowledge You
as the Giver of all good gifts.

Open us to give without counting the cost,
to share without expecting something in return.

Inspire us to be wise in ways of caring for ourselves and others,
to hold all our blessings and gifts with open hands,
to recognize the abundance of blessings in each new day.

Guide us to embrace the talents and skills You have given us
and use these in service of Your people in need.

Lead us to be happy with having what we need,
to be wise in distinguishing between our needs and our wants.

Give us each a servant's heart and hands,
that we may reflect Your love and kindness in all we do.

Amen

1. In this season of Thanksgiving, what blessings am I most grateful for in my life ?
2. What blessings in my life do I sometimes take for granted?

A Thanksgiving Blessing

May an abundance of gratitude burst forth as we reflect upon each of the blessings we enjoy.

May thanksgiving overflow in our hearts, and often be proclaimed in our prayer.

May we gather within the gladness of our hearts those special people who are faithful, kind, and gracious to us.

May our baskets of blessings always surprise us with their rich diversity of gifts and many opportunities to grow.

May we slow the hurried pace of life, so we can be aware of and enjoy what we sometimes take for granted.

May we be always open, willing, and ready to share our blessings with others.

May we give thanks everyday to our Generous and Gracious God, who loves each of us so lavishly and unconditionally.

Loving God, look upon us kindly this day. Fill our hearts and our world with peace.

Bless this food which has been prepared for us to enjoy together. Bless those who have prepared it and are serving us today. We ask this in your name. Amen

Gathering Prayer for December

Faithful and Ever-Present God,
You know all the things which fill our minds and hearts
during these busy and full days of this
Advent and Christmas Season.

Help us, in the midst of the scurry of activities,
to be attentive and aware of Your presence in our lives.

Open our hearts to experience Your presence and see You
in the faces of those we are called to serve,
in the eyes and efforts of those with whom we work,
in the midst of our family and community activities,
and in the invitations to help people in need
during this holiday season.

Guide us to be patient and understanding
toward our co-workers and all who come to us in need.

Bless each of our lives with inner peace and joy
as we celebrate the reason for this season.

You came to be God-with-us, to share in our humanity,
and invite us to be one with You.

Amen

1. Is there anything in my life which seems to hinder me from experiencing the inner peace and joy of this Advent and Christmas Season?
2. What are the best "gifts" which I could give and also receive in this holy Season?

A Christmas Prayer

Good and Gracious God,
as we celebrate this Christmas Season,
we thank You for the priceless gift You have given to us
in sending Jesus to walk among us on this earth.

Jesus has shown us Your great love and how we are to live.

May the green of our Christmas trees and holly remind us
of the eternal life and hope You give to each of us.

May the many bright colors of our decorations and packages
remind us of the rich variety of blessings

You shower upon us each day.

May the lights shining brightly on our trees and in our homes
remind us that You are always with us to light our path
in times of joy as well as in our darkness.

May the songs of the angels always be sung in our hearts
bringing Your Joy and Peace to our lives
and the lives of all we love and serve.

May the wonderful generosity and service
of all our families, friends, and co-workers
continue to be a sign of Your love and compassion among us,
in this Christmas Season and all through the year.

Amen

Letting God Speak to Us
in Times of Anxiety or Illness

There are times in our lives when we are too ill or cannot find words to pray. At times like these, it is good to just let God speak to us or let others read these words of comfort to us as we rest quietly with them. I once heard that there are 365 places in Scripture where God tells us, "Do not be afraid" or "Peace be with you". Some of these Scriptures are shared here as reassurance for you to hear. Let these words soak into your spirit and heart, to give you comfort as you rest.

After this, the word of the LORD came to Abram in a vision: "Do not be afraid, Abram. I am your shield, your very great reward. *Genesis 15:1*

That night the LORD appeared to him and said, "I am the God of your father Abraham. Do not be afraid, for I am with you." *Genesis 26:24*

Moses said to the people, "Do not be afraid. Stand firm and you will see the deliverance the LORD will bring you today." *Exodus 14:13*

See, the LORD your God has given you the land. Go up and take possession of it as the LORD, the God of your fathers, told you. Do not be afraid; do not be discouraged." *Deuteronomy 1:21*

Do not be fainthearted or afraid; do not be terrified or give way to panic. *Deuteronomy 20:3*

The LORD himself goes before you and will be with you; he will never leave you nor forsake you. Do not be afraid; do not be discouraged. *Deuteronomy 31:8*

Be strong and courageous, and do the work. Do not be afraid or discouraged, for the LORD God, my God, is with you. He will not fail you or forsake you. *1 Chronicles 28:20*

In God I trust; I will not be afraid. *Psalm 56:11*

The LORD is with me; I will not be afraid. *Psalm 118:6*

When you lie down, you will not be afraid; when you lie down, your sleep will be sweet. *Proverbs 3:24*

Be careful, keep calm and don't be afraid. Do not lose heart. *Isaiah 7:4*

Surely God is my salvation; I will trust and not be afraid. The LORD, the LORD, is my strength and my song; he has become my salvation. *Isaiah 12:2*

Do not be afraid, O little Israel, for I myself will help you, declares the LORD, your Redeemer, the Holy One of Israel. *Isaiah 41:14*

This is what the LORD says— he who made you, who formed you in the womb, and who will help you: Do not be afraid, O Jacob, my servant whom I have chosen. *Isaiah 44:2*

Do not tremble, do not be afraid. Did I not proclaim this and foretell it long ago? You are my witnesses. Is there any God besides me? No, there is no other Rock; I know not one. *Isaiah 44:8*

Do not be afraid. Since the first day that you set your mind to gain understanding and to humble yourself before your God, your words were heard, and I have come in response to them. *Daniel 10:12*

Do not be afraid. Peace! Be strong now; be strong. When he spoke to me, I was strengthened and said, "Speak, my lord, since you have given me strength." *Daniel 10:19*

I will save you, and you will be a blessing. Do not be afraid, but let your hands be strong. *Zechariah 8:13*

Even though I walk through the valley of the shadow of death, I will fear no evil, for you are with me; your rod and your staff, they comfort me. *Psalm 23:4*

My comfort in my suffering is this: Your promise preserves my life. *Psalm 119:50*

May your unfailing love be my comfort, according to your promise to your servant. *Psalm 119:76*

When you pass through the waters, I will be with you; and when you pass through the rivers, they will not sweep over you. When you walk through the fire, you will not be burned; the flames will not set you ablaze. *Isaiah 43:2*

You are precious and honored in my sight, and I love you. *Isaiah 43:4*

Do not be afraid, for I am with you. *Isaiah 43:5*

Shout for joy, O heavens; rejoice O earth; burst into song, O mountains! For the LORD comforts his people and will have compassion on his afflicted ones. *Isaiah 49:13*

I have seen his ways, and I will heal him; I will guide him and restore comfort to him. *Isaiah 57:18*

As a mother comforts her child, so will I comfort you. *Isaiah 66:13*

Then maidens will dance and be glad, young men and old as well. I will turn their mourning into gladness; I will give them comfort and joy instead of sorrow. *Jeremiah 31:13*

Blessed are those who mourn, for they will be comforted. *Matthew 5:4*

Then Jesus said to them, "Do not be afraid. Go and tell my brothers to go to Galilee; there they will see me." *Matthew 28:10*

But the angel said to him: "Do not be afraid, Zechariah; your prayer has been heard." *Luke 1:13*

But the angel said to her, "Do not be afraid, Mary, you have found favor with God." *Luke 1:30*

But the angel said to them, "Do not be afraid. I bring you good news of great joy that will be for all the people." *Luke 2:10*

Do not be afraid, little flock, for your Father has been pleased to give you the kingdom. *Luke 12:32*

Peace I leave with you; my peace I give you. I do not give to you as the world gives. Do not let your hearts be troubled and do not be afraid. *John 14:27*

Do not let your hearts be troubled. Trust in God; trust also in me. *John 14:1*

Praise be to the God and Father of our Lord Jesus Christ, the Father of compassion and the God of all comfort. *2 Corinthians 1:3*

God comforts us in all our troubles, so that we can comfort those in any trouble with the comfort we ourselves have received from God. *2 Corinthians 1:4*

For just as the sufferings of Christ flow over into our lives, so also through Christ our comfort overflows. *2 Corinthians 1:5*

If we are distressed, it is for your comfort and salvation; if we are comforted, it is for your comfort, which produces in you patient endurance of the same sufferings we suffer. *2 Corinthians 1:6*

And our hope for you is firm, because we know that just as you share in our sufferings, so also you share in our comfort. *2 Corinthians 1:7*

If you have any encouragement from being united with Christ, if any comfort from his love, if any fellowship with the Spirit, if any tenderness and compassion, then make my joy complete by being like-minded, having the same love, being one in spirit and purpose. *Philippians 2:1-2*

One night the Lord spoke to Paul in a vision: Do not be afraid; keep on speaking, do not be silent. *Acts 18:9*

Then he placed his right hand on me and said: Do not be afraid. I am the First and the Last. **I am the living one! I am alive forever and ever.** *Revelation 1:17-18*

Index

A Prayer for New Year's Day	p. 3
A Prayer for Caregivers	p. 21
A Prayer for Persons Sick or Injured	p. 175
A Prayer in Times of Uncertainty	p. 174
A Prayer for Trust	p. 173
A Prayer before Surgery	p. 170
A Prayer in Time of Illness	p. 172
A Mother's Prayer during Pregnancy	p. 169
A Prayer for Healers	p. 171
A Prayer for Nurses	p. 57
A Prayer for Doctors	p. 41
A Prayer for Healthcare Workers	p. 177
A Prayer of Gratitude for Mothers	p. 181
A Prayer of Gratitude for Fathers	p. 182
Morning Prayers	p. 178-179
Evening Prayers	p. 180
Prayer of St. Francis	p. 193
Week of Prayer for Christian Unity	p. 10 -13
World Day of Prayer for the Sick	p. 21
Prayers for the Season of Lent	p. 25-45
Prayers for the Easter Season	p. 46-52
A Prayer for Memorial Day	p. 66-67

A Prayer for 4th of July   p. 84

A Prayer for Labor Day   p. 113

A Veteran's Day Prayer   p. 143

A Thanksgiving Blessing   p. 195

Prayers for the Season of Advent   p. 150-162

A Prayer for St. Nick's Day   p. 155

A Christmas Prayer   p. 197

A New Year's Eve Prayer   p. 165

CPSIA information can be obtained
at www.ICGtesting.com
Printed in the USA
FFHW021402170419
51835751-57228FF